DOING BUSINESS GODS WAY

Learn the skills you will need to start
or grow a successful great business

KINGSTONE P. NGWIRA

authorHOUSE®

AuthorHouse™
1663 Liberty Drive
Bloomington, IN 47403
www.authorhouse.com
Phone: 833-262-8899

Published by AuthorHouse 12/03/2020

ISBN: 978-1-6655-0803-2 (sc)
ISBN: 978-1-6655-0804-9 (hc)
ISBN: 978-1-6655-0802-5 (e)

Library of Congress Control Number: 2020922587

Print information available on the last page.

Contents

Dedication

To the source of all true visions and sustainer of all dreams. To Bishop Solomon Adebayo, my faithful partner in vision. Your faith and belief in me and the vision over the years has encouraged me.

To all Entrepreneurs, Corporate Leaders and God's servants. God did not call the seed of Jacob in vain.

To all those men and women who do not quit when their ventures face corporate decline.

To my executive leadership team at Pentecostal Life Church International, thank you for your visionary support.

To my beloved wife Pastor Shannila, and my children Pastor Prince and Gift. Thanks for believing.

Acknowledgements

I would like to say a big thank you to all wonderful people who have worked so hard to make this edition a possibility. All staff at Great Dominion Holdings Limited (GDHL), Corporate Printing and Packaging Limited, Pentecostal Life University, Pentecostal Life FM and Great Dominion TV, Dominion Properties Limited (DPL), Dominion Foundation Limited (DFL), Corporate Investments Limited (CIL) and Great Entrepreneurship Club (GEC) have been wonderful. Thank you.

I must also commend all my associate pastors at Pentecostal Life Church International and all our staff. Your support, dedication and commitment are truly exceptional. My sincerely gratitude to my heartthrob and sweetheart Shannila and our children: Pastor Prince and Gift. You are my home team and I love and appreciate you. You are wonderful.

Preface

In the course of this book you will learn skills you need to start or grow a successful great business. You will learn the business growth strategies and how to implement them. What comes out clearly is that God has plans for you. They have been there before you were born, waiting for you to step into your assignment.

It is your duty to discover plans and steps into your divine assignment. So discover your God-given assignment and pursue it. Everyone God called, He gave a task to perform. For example he called Moses to deliver Israel from Egypt. Joshua was called to lead people to Canaan. He called David to be King and Jeremiah to be a prophet. Learning the skills for starting and growing a great successful business might of course be very intimidating and I fully recommend that you use your own mentor to help you through this process.

Let me pin point out that ideas rule the world. An idea to start and grow a successful great business is possible. Success is not a matter of luck or accident or being in the right place at the right time. Success is possible and by the practicing what you will learn from this book you will move to the front line in life. You will have an edge over those who do not know or who do not practice the techniques and strategies highlighted in this book.

Your own successful business can be many things. It can be your meal ticket, ensuring the economic health of you and your family. It can be your source of creativity, giving you an outlet for all those ideas you have. It can be your security, the comfort that comes from knowing that there is no boss who can fire you. It can even be your pride and joy, an accomplishment that you point to with satisfaction, knowing that you alone created it out of whole cloth.

But more than anything else, I think that owning your own business and being an entrepreneur is about freedom. Yes, the money that comes from a successful business is great. And yes, being energized and enthused about your day is special. Being free is priceless. If you do it right, you are free to start whatever sort of business you want.

You are free to start whatever sort of business you want. You are free to make as much money as you are capable of, without early limits or performance reviews. But you will notice that all this only comes about if you do it right. When you choose to become an entrepreneur, there are no guarantees. In large part, whether you succeed or fail is up to you. So, how do you do it right? Read this book. It is dedicated to helping you succeed. And unlike other start your own business books on the market, what sets this book apart is that it offers a model of business success, a simple model that is easily duplicated.

It goes without saying that if you consistently do the things that other successful people do, nothing in the world can stop you from becoming a great success yourself. You will now be the architect of your own destiny. After learning the practical skills to start and grow a great successful business you will be able to accomplish your goal. I am sure that thus book will give you a specific answer or a specific piece of advice on exactly what type of business you should start or how you should run your business, what this book will give you are the tools to be able to learn on your own as far as what type of business you should start, run and grow.

I also hope to help you understand the principles and concepts of starting and growing a successful great business and provide the practical tools and skills necessary to bring your vision into reality. You were born to achieve something significant and you were destined to make a difference in your generation. Your life is not a divine experiment but a project to providence to fulfill a purpose that your generation needs.

I therefore encourage you to believe in your dreams and trust God to commit it to delivery. This is a call not to be trapped in the folly of comparing yourself with others. Rather discover your individuality and accept your responsibility. Your future is not ahead of you- it lies within you. See beyond the nose and live for the unseen.

Kingstone P. Ngwira

Introduction

Success
Is not a destination it is a journey

WHAT YOU ARE ABOUT TO LEARN can change your life. So I would like to say congratulations for picking up this book. Get ready because your life is about to be drastically transformed. This book will not leave you where it found you. The ideas, insights and robust strategies presented in the entire write up have been the bedrock of starting or growing a successful great business. We are living at the greatest time in all human history where more people are becoming wealthy starting from nothing. You may wish to know that nearly more than 80 percent of financially successful people today started off broke or nearly broke.

Many business commentators say that a successful business life is not measured by the quantity of accumulated possession, neither is measured by popularity. But rather, it consists of the attainment of God's goals and purposes for one's life.

> **For I know the thoughts that I think toward you, saith the Lord, thoughts of peace, and not of evil, to give you an expected end:**
>
> Jeremiah 29:11

The living Bible presents it in this way: **For I know the plans I have for you, says the Lord. They are plans for good and not for evil, to**

give you a future and a hope. God has plans for you and they have been there waiting for you. Discover your God given a purpose or assignment on earth, pursue it and you will have a great successful. To run a successful great business requires good thinking and good thinkers are always In demand. Good thinkers solve problems, they never lack ideas that can build a successful great business and they always have hope for a better future. This book therefore is an indication of the thought process that I believe can lead people to start and grow a successful great business. It has worked for me and I believe it will also work for you.

> **That which was from the beginning which we have heard, which we have seen with our eyes, which we have looked upon and our hands have handled of the word of life.**
>
> 1 John 1:1

> **That which we have seen and heard declare we unto you that you also may have the fellowship with us and truly our fellowship is with the father and with his son Jesus Christ.**
>
> 1 John 1:3

The starting point in a starting business is get the basics right. Decide the type/business format of business you want to start: Sole proprietor under your name, Partnerships or Limited Liability companies. These have advantages and disadvantages. There is need to think of a business format. Decide on the name, product and service you will offer. You need to know why you want to start a business. You need to give more room for preparation. Ask yourself questions like am I ready to go own my own?

Do I have what it takes to go into business? Am I passionate to start my own business and to be my own boss? What are the skills, talents do I have. What skills and talents do I not have; am prepared to get additional training? Am I confident to continue business even if hard times come? After business failure will I give up? You need to deal with these questions upfront. Do I have support of my family and friends? It is important that they agree because at times you will use the family resources to build your business so you will need the family blessings to use them.

Be honest with yourself on what sacrifices you need to offer, what is it that you are passionate about otherwise you will fail. Don't go into a business just because you have money you will fail. There is more that is required than money alone. May be you are better working than to start your own business. Many businesses fail due to lack of preparation and planning.

Through wisdom is a house builded; and by understanding it is established.

Proverbs 24:3

Not everyone can run a business. Running a business requires resources such as money, energy, human capital, social life, losing some friends etc. You need to discipline yourself like working up early than anyone else, sacrificing your salary being last to be paid; if resources are not permitting. Put together a detailed business plan and some research about business product, customers,markets,competition, environment or the analyses. Count the cost; how much money you need to start the business. Starting a business requires money and it has financial implications. You cannot start a business without money. Thus why banks look for a contribution. However, you can start with what you have. It is advisable to go into business at an early age than an old age so that you prepare for succession planning.

Decide whether you will start from scratch or buy or in portion or franchise, or buy shares and owning 51% shares in an organization you own management control: Franchise-existing businesses instead of operating under a known brand with support systems : cannot come in and change systems: it's worth thinking of franchise though it has its own short comings.

Before you jump in, indeed before you do anything, you first must figure out if there is a market for your proposed business. The first law of business is (or at least should be): You must fulfill a market need. If there is no one around who wants or is willing to pay for your proposed product or service, your business will fail; it is as simple as that. So before you name the business or get a business license, or take out an advance on your credit card, you need to do some market research.

Market research will help you find out. Analyzing the market and industry is a way to gather facts about potential customers and determine the demand for your product or service. The more information you gather, the greater your chances of capturing a segment of the market. That is why you need to know your potential market before investing your time and money in any business venture. You don't want to waste time or money on a bad idea.

In essence, you must ask yourself whether anyone wants or needs your proposed business. In addition, it is equally important to research your potential competition and the industry in general, so you can have a good idea about what you are getting into. By figuring out your potential market, your likely competition, and how you will stand out from the crowd, you will greatly increase your chances of success.

In the process of taking the journey of starting or growing a successful great business which translates to wealth creation I have come to some critical conclusions I wish to share with you in this book: How to start a successful great business, how to start a successful great business, exploits in business and releasing your increase.

PART I

GETTING STARTED

CHAPTER 1

Business Overview

> "Dreams of today are
> the realities of tomorrow"

STARTING A SUCCESSFUL GREAT BUSINESS requires preparation, special talents, skills as well as resources. These are critical requirements before you step into any business. Experience and observation has shown that many businesses both great and small fail because of poor lack of preparation. You need to know that Prior Proper Performance Prevents Poor Performance.

So that I would like to say congratulations! The decision to start your own business can be one of the best you will ever make in your life. Owning your own business should be an exhilarating, inspiring, grand adventure; one full of new sights and experiences, delicious highs and occasional lows, tricky paths and hopefully, big open sky's. But to ensure that your business journey will be a fruitful one, it is important to understand all that becoming an entrepreneur entails.

Pros and Cons

Many people start their business adventure dreaming of riches and freedom. And while both are certainly possible, the first thing to understand is that there are tradeoffs when you decide to start a business. Difficult bosses, annoying coworkers, peculiar policies, demands upon your time and limits on how much money you can make are traded for independence, creativity, opportunity and power. But by the same token, you also swap a regular paycheck and benefits for no paycheck and no benefits. A life of security, comfort and regularity is traded for one of uncertainty.

There are definitely pros and cons to starting your own business. To be more precise, the benefits of starting a business include:

Control

Even if you like your boss and your job, the possibility remains that you can be laid off at any time. That boss you like so much can be transferred. Your Company can go bankrupt. So one advantage of starting your own business is that you are more in control of your work and career. And while that may be comforting, you should also realize that with that control will come increased responsibility and a new set of demands. As the boss, the buck must stop with you. You are the one who has to meet payroll. You are the one who has to make sure that clients and customers are happy. You are the one who must hire and fire the employees. It is not always easy and you can bet that there will certainly be times when you will look fondly back on your days as an employee, when you had far less responsibility and control.

Money

Many people choose to start their own business for the simple reason that they think that they are worth more money than they are making or they want the chance to provide a better life for their family. There is usually a limit to how much money you can make when you are an employee. The good news is that when you are the employer, the entrepreneur, the boss, there are far fewer limits. That can be a good or bad thing; you may make a fortune or you may go bust. If thus kind of uncertainty appeals to you, good, because it is what you will be getting if you start your own business.

Creativity and Independence

If you feel stagnant in your current job, you won't feel stagnant for long if you start a business. Running your own business may require you to be the marketing wizard, salesman, bookkeeper, secretary and president all rolled into one. It is a hectic life. But you may not mind that. It's kind of like the Calvin and Hobbes cartoon in which Calvin's mother tells him to make his bed. Calvin decides to build a robot to make the bed for him. when Hobbes asks, "Isn't making the robot more work than making the bed?" Calvin answers,

"It's only work if someone makes you do it!" The same holds true when the business is yours-it often doesn't feel like work because no one is making you do it.

Freedom

Working at your own business gives you the flexibility to decide when and where you will work. You decide your hours and place of business. The freedom that comes with being your own boss, where no one can tell you what to do or how to do it, may be the best thing about being an entrepreneur. But there are also downsides to starting your own business.

Uncertainty

As indicated, the life of an entrepreneur is not necessarily an easy one. Is it fun? Yes. Is it challenging, exciting, and spontaneous? You bet. But it is not easy. The hardest part of being in business for yourself is that there is no steady source of income; a paycheck does not come every two weeks.

Risk

What is an entrepreneur? An entrepreneur is someone who is willing to take a risk with money to make money. Not all entrepreneurial ventures are successful. The willingness to take a smart, calculated risk is the hallmark of a smart entrepreneur. But even calculated risks are still risks. You could make a million or you could go bankrupt.

Lack of structure

Many people like the structure of working for someone else. They know what is expected of them and what they need to accomplish each day. This is not true when you work for yourself. The work is very unpredictable. You need to consider carefully both the risks and rewards of entrepreneurship before deciding to jump in. It is easy to become infatuated with the idea of owning your own business. But if you are going to do it right, if you are going to do it right, if you are going to be successful, you need to take emotion out of the equation. You have to begin to think like a businessman, consider the risks and make an informed, intelligent, calculated decision.

Do You Have What It Takes?

Considering the pros and cons of this venture is not enough. Making the decision to leave your job and start a business is monumental. Even if starting a business seems like a great idea, despite the drawbacks, the question remains: How do you know if you are called by God to be an entrepreneur? Do you have what it takes? Business people come in all shapes and sizes, temperaments and skills levels. Thus, no test can determine if you are perfectly suited to be an entrepreneur. But analyzing these issues will help you realize some of the skills and competences necessary to start your own business. You will only be hurting yourself and your business if you pretend to have skills and competencies you don't possess.

Making the Decision

Deciding on area that you love is only the first step when choosing a business to start. The rest of the required analysis is much more left-brained, more analytical. It consists of two steps: Fist is looking at how much you have to invest and the last is conducting market research.

Analyzing Your Start-Up Costs

As important as it is to choose a business you will love, the business you pick must be one you can afford. While this book discusses many ways to get the money you will need to start your business, you probably already have a fairly good idea how much you will need to start your business, you probably already have a fairly good idea how much you will have to get started. Needless to say, the business you choose must fit within those parameters.

Essentially, there are two types of businesses: service based businesses and product based businesses. Of the two, service businesses and product based businesses. Of the two, service businesses are far less expensive to start. If you open an accounting firm, for example, all you may need to get started is letterhead, an office, and a computer. On the other hand, if you want to start a computer store, you need to have inventory, shelving, and fixtures and display cases, not to mention retail space, a security system a sales staff. One of the first things you must do is analyze your start-up costs to determine.

Conducting Market Research

The other aspect of choosing the right business is making sure 5that there is a need for the business you want to start. There are few things worse in than putting a lot of money, time, and effort into creating a new business, only to find that there is no market for what you are selling. The important thing is that you choose a business that fits your personality, is something you love and can be successfully implemented with the resources available to you. If that means scaling your idea back a bit in the beginning, that's fine. Once you get your baby off the ground, you can grow.

CHAPTER 2

Preparation in Getting the Basics Right for Starting a Great Successful Business

> "People become Successful the minute they decide to"

PREPARATION

In Ecclesiastes 3, we are told that there is a time for everything. You have to ask God *"when"* for your assignment. God knows the perfect time for you to set out. Moses in the book Exodus struck for 40 years earlier than God's time. This sent him on personal exile, he was downgraded. Jesus, the son of God, was the natural son of Joseph for 30 years, until He became into the fullness of time.

> **For which of you intending to build a tower sitteth not down first and counteth the cost whether he have sufficient to finish it.**
>
> Luke 14:28

> **Lest haply after he hath laid the foundation and is not able to finish it all that behold it begin to mock him saying this man began to build and was not able to finish.**
>
> Luke 14:29-30

During the preparation time is when you need to set goals and proper planning in terms of required resources and setting priorities. There is what is called "the fullness of time". It is the right time to step out into your God given assignment after a good preparation. You need to be sensitive to the right time, in order to make healthy progress. So prepare before stepping out into your great business and you will succeed.

AMBITION

This is one's expectation or what one looks forward to achieving. Thus, it is a self –made plan. Nothing is practicing wrong with good ambitious. But, "without vision the people perish". Ambition is therefore liable to failure and can even destroy the ambitious one. Only the ambition that falls in line with God's drawn-out plan becomes fruitful and successful. Absalom was ambitious and his ambition killed him!

Dr. David Oyedepo says "ambition says, I want it by all means", but vision says, "I have it because God says it, and I am in his plan". Ambition is the brother of anxiety, whereas vision is a relative of peace.

TALENTS, SKILLS, COMPETENCIES AND ABILITIES

Special talents, skills, competencies and abilities are required for you to achieve your goal, impressions and ambitions of owning or running a successful great business. This is a call to clarify them and craft superior strategies to multiply and maximize them.

When clarifying them you need to develop absolute clarity about what who you are, what you want and the best way to achieve it. This leads to multiplication of your talents, skills, competences and abilities from which you leverage yourself and other people's customers, knowledge, ability, efforts, money and resources.

To achieve this comes the need to determine your special talents, skills, competencies, abilities and strengths and focus on developing them to a higher level.

BECOME A GREAT LEADER

Starting or growing a successful business requires you to become a great leader. Your personal leadership ability is the major limit on what you can achieve. Leadership is the major factor for business success. Leadership is the ability to get results through influence and this requires having a clear vision of the future of your great business and take courage to take action with no guarantee success.

Responsibilities of leadership include setting and achieving business goals, market and innovate-continuously seek faster, better, cheaper, easier ways to creative and keep customers, set priorities and work on key tasks while supervising results. Additionally, leadership also involves solving problems, making decisions, leading by example, perform and get results.

EFFECTIVE MANAGEMENT OF RESOURCES

To run a successful great business requires effective management of a variety of resources such as great people, equipment, property, cash, great product or service and inventory. Of all these resources cash is probably the most important. With sufficient cash a business has the ability to buy any of the other resources in which it may be deficient.

Whether the purchase of that resource is worthwhile at the price required is another matter, but the purchase can still be made. All the resources other than cash have a value to business that is dependent on their availability, utilization, market demand and prevailing economic climate. It is cash and only cash that maintains a constant value and can easily be turned into other assets or resources.

CONFIRMATION

This is seeking the affirmation of others in deciding what steps to take in starting your great business. God is never moved by multitudes or by popular opinion. If all the prophets in the world prophesy you into a successful great business and God has not ordained that business will fail.

I have not sent these prophets yet they run. I have not spoken to them yet they prophesy

Jeremiah 23:21

Many people are running a race they have not assigned to run and results failure. If you go into the business that God has not confirmed or ordained be assured that you will finance that business yourself. So stop being led by men, rather, be led by God. If you let God lead you, ten you shall not want! No amount of confirmation by people can put words into his mouth. What he has not said; what he has not written, he has not written. Locate his writing about you, not writings of men. Human confirmation is, more often than not, confusion is disguise.

CHOOSING GREAT NAMES AND LOCATIONS

Now that you have a good idea about what your business is going to be and where you are headed with it, it is to begin to put your foundation in place. You will need to structure the business legally, get the necessary licenses and permits, and get funding. But before you can do any of those things, it is time to have some fun. You need name your business and, in all likelihood, find a location for it. Remember Location, Location and Location.

What's in a Name?

Naming your business should be enjoyable, but for some people, it is stressful. W2hat if you pick the wrong name? What if the name you pick has already been taken? While it is smart to be cautious, it is nothing to get overly concerned about. The important thing to realize is that your business name will become your alter ego, so be sure to pick a name that reflects on you and your business well. How do you pick a name? You have three options.

The first is to pick a name that says exactly what your business is. Begin with what your business is going to do and the image you want to express. Include both in the actual name of the business or reflect those ideas in the name, so that when people hear your business name, they know what you are offering. Be sure the name is not already in local use and that it is not too similar to that of a competitor. Try to pick one that is catchy and memorable; alliteration often works well. Also, be sure to pick a name that is not difficult to pronounce or spell. When people call directory assistance, you want them to be able to find you. After you come up with five names that you really like, get some feedback from people you trust; they may not think your name is as good as you think it is. Remember, your business has to serve a market need, so finding out what the market things about your proposed business name, even in a small and informal way, is smart.

The second method of business-name creation is to pick a name that is totally unique and has nothing to do with your business at all. Choose names that are great because they are so unique that they are memorable. The risk here is that while your name may be unique, it may be too odd and obscure foe people to remember it.

Trademark Concerns

While making your final decision regarding your name, it is important to do a trademark search to see if the name already has been trademarked. If it has, you may not be able to use it. Different names are given different degrees of trademark protection.

A trademark is a distinctive word, phrase, or logo that is used to identify a business. Nike and its unique swoosh symbol are protected under trademark law because they are distinctive. Other words are given far less protection. Common or ordinary words that are not inherently distinctive get much less, or no, trademark protection, even if someone tries to trademark them.

Licenses, Permits, and Business Formation

Deciding what legal form your business should take is not the most scintillating of topics, but it may be one of the most important decisions you will make. The form your business takes can determine how big it may grow, who can invest in it, and who is responsible should it get in trouble. It is a critical decision. Once decided, it is then important to handle some other legal, namely getting the requisite licenses and permits required by your city, country or state.

BUSINESS FORMATION

There are three forms your business can take. It can be a sole proprietorship, a partnership or a corporation and each of the last two have subsets. When deciding which of these is best for you, it would behoove you to speak with both your lawyer and your account, because each choice has different legal and financial considerations to weigh. Below is an overview that you can use as a launching pad for discussions with your own advisors.

Sole proprietorships and General Partnerships

A sole proprietorship is the cheapest and easiest form of business you can start. Simply decide on a name for your business, get a business license, file and publish a fictitious business name statement, hang your shingle, and voila! You are in business.

The downside to sole proprietorship to significant: You and the business are legally the same thing. If something goes wrong, say as a chiropractor you accidentally injure someone, not only is your business at risk, but so are your personal assets. Your home, cars, bank accounts, everything at risk when you are a sole proprietor. Another problem with the form of business is that you have no partners to work with or bounce ideas off of. It is a dangerous way to do business Therefore, having a teammate is why operating a business as a partnership is attractive.

Essentially, a business partnership is a lot like a marriage. You need to pick a good partner because you will be spending a lot of time together and trusting each other. And, as with a sole proprietorship, in a general partnership, both you and your partner are personally liable for the debts of the business. The danger is that your partner can make some dumb decisions and get the partnership into debt and you will be personally responsible for that debt. So as you can see, while there are many good aspects to having a partner, partnerships are fraught with danger. You have to weigh the benefits against the burdens and decide if bringing in a partner is right for you.

Another thing to be wary of is the emotional aspect of having a partner. One advantage to being a sole proprietor, and thus the only boss, is you have no one to answer to except yourself. That's one of the definite perks of being a solo entrepreneur. Bringing in a partner means you will have to consider another point of view before any major decision is made. Also, when partnerships do not work out, best friends who become partners do not always stay best friends.

On the other side of the ledger, there are many things to be said for having a business partner. One is that it enables you to have someone with whom to brainstorm. That great idea you have may not be such a great idea after all, and a partner you trust can tell you why. A partner also gives you another pair of hands to do the work. It is difficult to be the one who has to do everything when you are solo. Partners alleviate that. Last, and certainly not least, having a business partner gives you someone to share the financial responsibilities of the business. That is not insignificant.

Having considered the pros and cons, having concluded that a partner can help more than it might hurt and maybe even knowing someone you would like to partner with, it is still a good idea that you "date" first before jumping in. Find a project or two and work together. See how you get along, how your style mesh (or don't), how you deal with deadlines and whether the union enhances your work. Remember, you will be spending a lot of time with your partner, so you need to be sure that you work well together, have a good time and have skills that complement one another.

Finally, get some work references and make some phone calls. Deciding to partner with someone is one of the most important decisions you can make in your small business, so don't skimp on the homework. As far as the costs go, the licensing and permits are fairly insignificant. The main cost is hiring a business lawyer to draft the partnership agreement.

Limited Partnerships

There are two classes of partnerships (discussed above) and limited partnerships. In a general, all partners are equal. Each partner has equal power to incur obligations on behalf of the partnership and each partner has unlimited liability for the debts of that partnership. Because not all partnerships require that the partnerships require that the partners have equal power and liabilities, some partnerships decide to form as a limited partnership instead. In a limited partnership, there is usually only one general partner (although there could be more). There other partners are called limited, hence the name limited partnership.

In a limited partnership, the general partner or partners have full management responsibility and control of the partnership business on a day to day basis. The general partner runs the show and makes the decisions.

A limited partner cannot incur obligations on behalf of the partnership and does not participate in the daily operations and management of the partnership and does not participate in the daily operations and management of the partnership. In fact, the participation of a limited partner in the partnership is usually nothing more than initially contributing capital and hopefully later receiving a proportionate share of the profits. A limited partner is essentially a passive investor.

While the general partner has all of the power, he or she also has the lion's share of the liability. A limited partner's liability is capped at the amount of his or her financial contribution to the partnership. Should the track of a limited partnership kill someone accidentally, the damaged party could go after the general partner's personal, but would be limited to the limited partner's contribution. Thus, then main advantage to this business entity is that it allows the general partner the freedom to run the business without interference, and gives the limited partners diminished liability if things go wrong.

Although a limited partner may seek to be more involved in the day-to-day operations of the partnership, he or she does so at some risk. If he or she does participate more, it is altogether possible that he or she may be viewed as a general partner in the eyes of the law, with its attendant liability risks. Another key benefit of the limited partnership is that it pays no income tax. Income and losses are attributed proportionally to each partner and accounted for on their respective tax returns

Because of this flow-through tax treatment, a limited partnership is often the structure of choice for real estate ventures and investment securities groups. If you do decide to start your business as a limited partnership, have your partnership agreement drafted by an attorney.

Incorporating

The best thing about forming your business as a corporation is that it limits your personal liability, which is not true for partnerships and sole

13

proprietorships. For example, say that you owned a tire shop and one of your employees negligently installed a tire that fell off a car and caused a three-car accident with several personal injuries. If your tire store was not a corporation, the injured parties could come after you for monetary damages.

This means that you could lose your business, your house everything. That would not be true if you incorporated. Creditors are limited to the assets of the corporation only for payment and may not collect directly from the shareholders. There are several types' corporations including limited liability companies, closely held corporations, professional corporations and S and C corporations.

Outfitting the office

The actual process of setting up your business will involve dealing with plenty of details -details that must be understood and organized before you open the doors; details that must be handled and forgotten so that you can go onto other, more important matters; details that sink or swim your business.

Automating Your Office

Whatever your business, you must computerize it. Whether it involves tracking sales, writing letters, or inventory control, starting out with a good computer system is vital. Although it may seem less expensive to do certain office tasks by hand rather than investing in a good computer system or related software, that is fuzzy logic for two reasons.

First, you eventually will automate whatever tasks you begin by hand. Changing over later will take longer and cost more. Second, computer hardware and software will allow you to be more effective and, thus, more productive from the get-go. Computers represent a solid investment of your start-up capital. Don't skimp in this area.

Throughout this book you have been, and will be cautioned to keep your overhead low. High overhead will eat up your profits and your precious cash flow quickly. But this is not one of those times. The rapid pace of technological change means that computers usually become obsolete within three or four years.

If you buy a used one, or an older or slower model, you are simply speeding up the moment when you will have to buy a new one. Be smart and buy a good computer and the necessary software now. You have likely learned a thing or two about purchasing computers since you brought your first one. You are more knowledgeable about your computer needs and your probably know what areas you would like to improve. It may be that your monitor is too small and you want a larger one, or that you want a newer operating system. Probably what you want is speed and more speed.

Creating a Great Image

At the night of the e-commerce boom, an executive from a well established "old-company" company was hired to be the new CEO of a young, brash, well-financed internet start-up. For his first day at his new company, the CEO decided to look his best. He dressed in an expensive suit and his favorite tie. That day, he was to address the company's 100-plus employees. As he tells the story, he felt sharp, and looked great. The new CEO gave an enthusiastic, short introductory speech and then opened the floor to questions. The room was utterly and completely silent. Seconds seemed like hours as people refused to participate. "Come on," he implored, "ask me a question," Finally, some yelled out, "Why are you wearing a tie?"

As in life, first impressions are awfully important in business too. After someone encounters you and your business for the first time, they will leave with an impression. It may be positive; it may be negative. They may think yours is a well-run, professional enterprise that will provide them with a great service, or not. One thing you can bank on though is that the first impression will very likely be the lens that they use to view your company forever.

Think about it in your own life. If you meet someone for the first time and he acts like a real jerk, don't you label him a jerk? It doesn't matter that he might have been having a bad day. He becomes "the jerk". When you go to a business for the first time and get bad service, don't you usually conclude that their business doesn't deserve your continued patronage? That is why they say that you only have one chance to make a great first impression.

The Importance of a Great Image

Although image isn't everything, it is not insignificant. Your signs, business cards, letterhead, logo and store /office say much about who you are. Combined, these things constitute your business identity. A professional business identity says that, even though you are new, you are to be taken seriously. Of course, you will have to back up that great image with great products or services and customer services. But to get people to understand that yours is a business worth patronizing, you have to open the door by having a sharper image. That is the task before you.

Your logo

A logo is one of the first things you need to create because it will be used on your letterhead, business cards and other documents. It will distinguish your company, set a tone, and foster your desired image. You want a logo that exemplifies who you are and what it is you do. When creating a logo, you have two options: you can do it yourself or hire someone to do it for you. If you decide to design your own logo. It is important that you will not use any material that is copyrighted in your logo design. If you can afford to hire someone to create a logo for you, do it.

Elements of Your Image

These items need to be coordinated and thematic in order to create a dynamic business identity and image:

Your Brochure

Not every business will need or use a brochure. Even if a brochure is not traditionally part of businesses like yours, it still might be a great way to create a professional image and bring in business. The thing to be wary of is spending money on a brochure if it really does nothing to add to your business. A brochure can be an expensive item and thus not worth the money if you really don't need it.

When creating a brochure, avoid the following:

Making it too busy. Creating a brochure that is so jam-packed with information that is unpleasing to the eye and difficult to read is a sure way to waste money. It is much better to keep paragraphs short, use whitespace, use bullets, and keep it simple.

Making the cover boring. Too many businesses think that headlining their brochure with their business name is a sure way to entice people to read more. If you want people to read your brochure, you must catch their attention (usually with some benefit they could get by reading more) and draw them in.

Ask yourself: What is the purpose of this brochure? Is it an introduction to your business, a selling tool, both, or more? Whatever your answer, your brochure needs to reflect the same values, tone and theme that will be found in your other image-creating materials. Use your logo. Use your colors. Reinforce your desired image with text and graphics that reflect your business image.

Signs

A big, bold, visible sign in the right location(s) can be one of the best tools for creating an image, as well as generating new business. Sign are obviously most used for retail businesses, especially when drop-traffic is a key element to your business model. Signs come in many forms, from cheap wood ones to expensive electrical and glass models. The same considerations that are used in your other materials apply here.

If you can get the image of each of your materials to reinforce an overall theme, busy people who don't yet know of your business will easily understand what will easily understand what it is you are about if they are met with consistency. Choosing the right sign especially is an area where professional expertise is useful. How big should the sign be? What should it say? How big should the letters be? Creative and design companies will help you figure this all out.

Your Website

Even if your business has nothing to do with the internet, you cannot pass up the chance to create an online image. Indeed, a website has become a business necessity. Not only is it an expensive way to buttress your image and tell people who you are, but it is also an opportunity to sell more, get more customers, make more money, and impress more strangers. And you need not be Amazon.com to be successful. In fact, you probably don't want to be.

Your business website should, in all likelihood, be a clean, simple, elegant place that does a few things very well. Your home page should explain what your business is and what the website is about. It should be simple and easy to load. Inside, your business addresses and contact information should be easy to find. Features and benefits of working with you should be prominent. Beyond that, what you do with your site is up to you.

You may want to consider having some features that keep people coming back, because the more they come back to your site, the more likely it is they will buy from you.

You can offer such things as:

Interactivity

E-commerce interactivity means providing interactive tools that enable potential customers to learn more about your products. It could also mean offering chartrooms, message boards, or newsletters. Streaming video is a possibility.

Members Only Areas

Some businesses offer members only domains on their websites, where they offer access to premium information, tools and services. Think about AOL for a moment. It is nothing but a huge member only website; not a bad model.

Content

On the internet, content is king. A site without good, arresting, useful, timely content is a site that is probably going nowhere. Think about the sites you like. What is it that draws you there? In all likelihood, good content is near the top of your list. Where do you get your content? You can write it yourself or hire someone to create content for you.

CHAPTER 3

Take a Business as a Calling

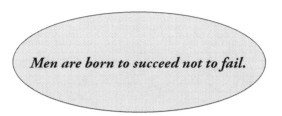

Men are born to succeed not to fail.

TAKING BUSINESS AS A CALLING simply means doing what you were born to do. This could be a process of discovering your purpose by reading books, listening to tapes, watching videos and attending seminars-studying successful people and establishing why and how they succeed. In pursuit of this you may learn that those who succeed re no better qualified than yourself. You may be shocked that the big difference could be that you are capable of doing and not the things you really wanted to do.

The key to life is discovery of a clear personal purpose a sense of destiny and a vision that motivates. Colossians 4:17says: **Say to Achipus take heed to the ministry which thou received in the lord that thou fulfill it.** From the above scripture it shows that failure to identify yourself with your purpose could lead you to invest in wrong areas of investments and that can lead to frustration. Taking business as a calling starts with beginning with the right environment. Just as each of us has a unique figure print you are also born with a unique purpose that only you can fulfill.

Start creating the environment for your purpose to be developed, matured and revealed to mankind. It is worth noting the words of Emile Bissel, "Great thoughts speak only to the thought mind, but great actions speak to all mankind." In many cases you will grow through a period of soul searching before your purpose will be revealed to you.

> **Wherefore the rather brethren give diligence to make your calling and elections sure for if ye do these things ye shall never fail.**
>
> 2 Peter 1:10

And with the realization that you can identify that a baby is a human being, but cannot know what it will become one day, you will know when you have found your purpose, but will not know how it will fulfilled.

> **Commit your works to the Lord and your plans will be established.**
>
> Proverbs 16:3

The how will always come later. The most important thing right now is to have a dream which you need to commit it to God to affect the delivery.

> **The mind of man plans his way, but the Lord directs his steps.**
>
> Proverbs 16:9

Your great business is inched in discovering your purpose which is directly linked with your talents, skills and abilities. Your purpose or calling is eagerly waiting for the right environment to generate and reveal itself to the world. This is a call to join the dreamer's world. Allow you to imagine and fantasize about the kind of business and life you would like to have. Think about the money you would like to earn as a return on your investment. You may wish know that great men and women begin with a dream of something wonderful and different from what they have today.

Brian Tracy calls this practice "back from the future" thinking. This is a powerful technique practiced continually by high performing men and women. This way of thinking has an amazing effect on your mind and on your behavior. Here is how it works: Project yourself forward five years. Imagine that five years have passed and that your life is now perfect in every respect.

What does it look like? What are you doing? How much money are having in the bank? What kind of life do you have?

Create a vision for yourself for the long-term future. The clearer your vision of healthy, happiness and prosperity, the faster you move forward it moves toward you.

> **Where there is no vision, the people perish: but he that keepeth the law, happy is he.**
>
> Proverbs 29:18

When you a create mental picture of where you are going in life, you become more positive, more motivated and more determined to make it a reality. You trigger your natural creativity and come up with idea to help make your vision come true.

You always tend to move in the direction of your dominant dreams: the images and visions. The very act of allowing yourself to dream big dreams actually raises your self esteem and causes you to like and respect yourself more. This in return improves your self-concept and increases your level of self confidence. It also increases your personal level of self respect and happiness.

CHAPTER 4

Create a Clear Vision and Mission for Your Business

If you do not have a vision of your own you will spend your life fulfilling other people's visions

GOD HAS A PLAN for everyone including you. Remember what I presented in earlier chapters:

> **"For I know the plans I have for you, says the Lord. They are plans for good and not for evil, to give you a future and a hope"**
>
> Jeremiah 29:11

You are not created to roam about in life purposely. You are designed for a specific placement. Before you were born, He knew you and separated you for a specific purpose goal and assignment. But your placement in the grand master plan of God is located by vision.

Strategic Vision is a description of the Road Map Having three questions: Where are we? Where do we want to be? How do we get there? Therefore, your views and conclusions about the businesses' long term direction is what constitute a strategic vision. There is no escaping the need for a strategic vision. Armed with a clear well-conceived business course for your business to follow, managers have a beacon to guide resource allocation and a basis for crafting a strategy to get the company where it needs to go.

Businesses whose managers neglect the task of thinking strategically about the company's future business path are prone to drift aimlessly and lose any claim to being an industry leader. On the other hand, a business's mission statement is typically focused on its present business scope:" who we are and what we do". For you and everyone to perform at highest level require a mission statements broadly describe businesses present capabilities, customer focus, activities and business makeup.

Establishing mission statement based on core values is equivalent to digging a foundation to your building. The difference between strategic vision and mission statement is that a mission statement speaks to what a company is doing today while strategic vision generally ha much greater direction -setting and strategy-making value mission statement has two questions: In what business are we in? and why are we in business. The question why are we in business leads to objectives of the business. Business objectives involve converting the strategic vision into specific performance targets outcomes for the company to achieve. The purpose of setting objectives is to convert managerial statements of strategic vision and business mission into specific performance targets-results and outcomes the organization wants to achieve.

Setting objectives and then measuring whether they are achieved or not help managers track an organization's progress. Managers of the best performing companies tend to set objectives that require stretch and disciplined effort. The challenge of trying to achieve bold, aggressive performance targets pushes an organization to be more inventive, to exhibit some urgency in improving both its financial performance (financial objectives) and business position (strategic objectives) and to be more intentional and focused in its actions.

CHAPTER 5

Develop a Great Product or Service

> *Work as though you would*
> *live forever and live as though*
> *you would die today*

THE QUALITY OF YOUR PRODUCT OR SERVICE determines 90% of business success. Quality is the key determinate of your growth and profitability. It is determinate of your reputation. How often customers say: "This is a great product or service!"

To this end you need to decide what exactly you intend to sell. Some questions include: what does your customer consider value and is willing to pay for it? What will be the best compliments that you receive from your happy customer? What will your products offer to your customers that make them superior to your competitors? What products or services should you abandon or discontinue because you cannot achieve excellence in those areas? The market only rewards for excellent products and services.

Although production is necessary economic activity, some people overrate its importance in relation to marketing. Production and marketing are both important parts of a total business system aimed at providing consumers with need-satisfying goods and services. Simply put take out marketing there will be no production. Together, production and marketing supply five kinds of economic utility:

Form Utility

Form utility is provided when someone produces something tangible (things you can touch or see).

Task Utility

Task utility is provided when someone performs a task for someone else. Thus, marketing decisions focus on the customer and include decisions about what goods and services to produce. It doesn't make sense to provide goods and services consumers don't want when they are so many things they do want.

Marketing is concerned with what customer's want- and should guide what is produced and offered. Even when marketing and production combine to provide form or task utility, consumers won't be satisfied until possession; time and place utility are also provided.

Possession Utility

Possession Utility means obtaining a good or service and having the right to use or consume it.

Time Utility

Time utility means having the product available when the customer wants.

Place Utility

Means having the product available where the customer wants.

CHAPTER 6

Craft a Great Business Plan

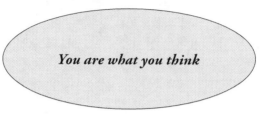

You are what you think

YOUR ABILITY TO PLAN AND ORGANIZE every detail of your great business is essential to your success and profitability. A good business plan must contain values: clear, core principles: Vision: ideal picture of the future of the business, mission: goals to accomplish, purpose: reasons why business exists, excellent leadership and management, excellent products and services, excellent reputation in market and solid financials.

Crafting a good business plan requires thinking and the quality of your thinking about the key elements of your business has the greatest impact of all on your success and needs you to answer questions like what are the core values and the principles that you and your business stand for and believe in? If your business was perfect in every way, what would it look like in future? What is your mission for your business defined in terms of how you would want to change or improve the life or work of your customers?

Solid Business plans don't guarantee success. But for entrepreneurs with decent ideas, they surely boost the odds. A good plan accomplishes three important tasks. First, it aligns the management team toward a common set of goals. Then, once the vision is on paper, it forces the teams to take a long, hard work at the feasibility of the business. "A business plan is like a dry run to see if there is a major problem with your business before losing any money," says Mike Mckeever, author of How to write a business plan. Finally, a business plan is a sales document: it aims to attract professional investors who may only have time for cursory glance at each idea that crosses their desks.

Here, then, are some highlights of an effective business plan. Start with a clear, concise executive summary of your business. Think of it like an elevator pitch. In no more than two pages, billboard all the important stuff. At the top, communicate your value proposition: what your company does how it will make money and why customers will want to pay for your product or service. If you are sending your plan to investors, include the amount of money you need and how you plan to use it. You so tackle the summary after finishing the rest of your plan.

Next, establish the market opportunity. Answer questions like: How large is your target market? How fat is it growing? Where are the opportunities and threats, and how will you deal with them? Again, highlight your value proposition. Most of this market information can be found through industry associations, chambers of commerce, census data or even from other business owners. (Be sure to source all of your information in case you are asked to back up your claims or need to update your business plan.)

While you may have convinced yourself that your product or service is unique, don't fall into the trap. Instead, get real and size of the competition: Who are they? What do they sell? How much market share do they have? Why will customers choose your product or service instead of theirs? What are the barriers to entry? Remember to include indirect competitors -those with similar capabilities that currently cater to a different market but could choose to challenge you down the road.

Now that you've established your idea, start addressing the execution -specifically, your team. Include profiles of each of your business's founders, partners or officers and what kinds of skills, qualifications and accomplishments they bring to the table. (Include, resumes in an appendix). If potential investors have read this far, it's time to give them the nuts and bolts of your business model. This includes a detailed description of all revenue streams (product sales, advertising, services, licensing) and the company's cost structure (Salaries, rent, inventory, and maintenance). Be sure to list all assumptions and provide a justification for them. Also, include names of key suppliers or distribution partners.

After all of that, one big question still remains: Exactly how much money does your business stand to make? More important, when will the cash come in the door? That's why you need a section containing past financial performance (If your company is a going concern) and financial projections. Three-year forward-looking profit and loss, balance sheet and cash flow statements are a must-as is a break-even analysis that shows how much revenue you need to cover your initial investment.

For early stage companies with only so much in the bank, the cash-flow statement comparing quarterly receivables to payables is most critical. "Everyone misunderstands cash flow," says Tim Berry, president of business-plan software company Palo alto Software" People think that if they plan for (accounting) profits, they'll have cash flow. But many companies that go under are profitable when they die, because profits aren't cash."

After you've buffed you plan to a shine, don't file it away to gather dust. "A Business plan is the beginning of a process, says Berry. "Planning is like steering and steering means constantly correcting errors. The plan itself holds just a piece of the value; it's the going back and seeing where you were wrong and why that matters."

Further, before coming up with a winning business plan you need to ask yourself the following questions: How long should the business plan be? When should you write it? Who needs a business plan? Why should you write a business plan? After answering these questions, you need to determine your goals and objectives, outline your financing needs, plan what you'll do with your plan and of course don't forget about marketing.

A great business plan should consist of the following sections:

Executive Summary

Within the overall outline of the business plan, the executive summary will follow the title page. The summary should tell the reader what you want. This is very important. All too often, what the business owner desires is buried on page eight. Clearly state what you're asking for in the summary.

Business Description

The business description usually begins with a short description of the industry. When describing the industry, discuss the present outlook as well as future possibilities. You should also provide information on all the various markets within the industry, including any new products or developments that will benefit or adversely affect your business.

Market Strategies

Market strategies are the result of meticulous market analysis. A market analysis forces the entrepreneur to become familiar with all aspects of the market so that the target market can be defined and the company can be positioned in order to garner its share of sales.

Competitive Analysis

The purpose of the competitive analysis is to determine the strengths and Weaknesses of the competitors within your market, strategies that will provide you with a distinct advantage, the barriers that can be developed in order to prevent competition from entering your market, and any weaknesses that can be exploited within the product development cycle.

Design & Development Plan

The purpose of this design and development plan section is to provide investors with a description of the product's design, chart its development within the context of production, marketing and the company itself, and create a development budget that will enable the company to reach its goals.

Operations & Management Plan

The operations and management plan are designed to describe just how the business functions on a continuing basis. The operations plan will highlight the logistics of the organization such as the various responsibilities of the management team, the tasks assigned to each division within the company, and capital and expense requirements related to the operations of the business.

Financial Factors

Financial data is always at the back of the business plan, but that doesn't mean it's any less important than up-front material such as the business concept and the management team.

WHAT MAKES A GOOD PLAN?

What factors are involved in creating a good business plan? Is it length of the plan? The information it covers? How well its written or the brilliance of its strategy. The following illustration shows a business plan as part of a process. You can think the good or bad of a plan as the plan itself, measuring its value by its contents.

There are some qualities in a plan that makes it more likely to create results, and these are important. However, it is even better to see the plan as part of the whole process of results, because even a great plan is wasted if nobody follows it,

A business plan will be hard to implement unless it is simple and, specific, realistic and complete. Even if it is all these things, a good plan will need someone to follow up and check on it. The plan depends on the human elements around it, particularly the process of commitment and involvement, and the tracking and the following up that comes afterward.

Successful implementation starts with a good plan. There are elements that will make a plan more likely to be successfully implemented.

Some of the clues to implementation include:

1. Is the plan simple? Is it easy to understand and to act on? Does it communicate its contents easily and practically?
2. Is the plan specific? Are their objectives concrete and measurable? Does it include specific date of completion, specific person's responsible and specific budgets?
3. Is the plan realistic? Are the sales goals, expense budgets and milestones date realistic? Nothing stifles implementation like unrealistic goals.

4. Is the plan complete? Does it include all the necessary elements? Requirements of a business plan vary, depending on the context. There is no guarantee, however, that the plan will work if it doesn't cover the main bases.

5. Too many people think of business plans as something you do to start a company, apply for a loan, or find investors. Yes, they are vital for those purposes, but there's a lot more to it. Preparing a business plan is an organized, logical way to look at all of the important aspects of a business.

First, decide what will use the plan for, such as to:

• Define and fix objectives and programs to achieve those objectives.
• Create regular business review and course correction.
• Define a new business.
• Support a loan application.
• Define agreements between partners.
• Set a value o n a business for sale or legal purposes.
• Set a value on a business for sale or legal purposes.
• Evaluate a new product line, promotion or expansion.

No time to plan? A common misconception

"Not enough time for a plan" business people say. "I can't plan. I'm too busy getting things done". A business plan now can save time and stress later.

Too many businesses make business plans only when they have to. Unless a bank or investors want to look at a business plan, there isn't likely to be a plan written. The busier you are, the more you need to plan. If you are always putting out fires, they should build fire breaks or a sprinkler system. You can lose the whole forest for too much attention to the individual trees.

KEYS TO BETTER BUSINESS PLANS

1. Use a business plan to set concrete goals, responsibilities and deadlines to guide your business.
2. A good business plan assigns tasks to people or departments and sets milestones and deadlines for tracking implementation.
3. A practical business plan includes 10 parts implementations for very one-part strategy.
4. As part of the implementation of a business plan, it should provide a forum for regular review and course corrections.
5. Good business plans are practical.
6. Don't use a business plan to show how much you know about your business.
7. Nobody reads a long-winded business plan: not bankers, bosses, nor venture capitalists. Years ago, people were favorably impressed by long plans. Today, nobody is interested in a business plan more than 50 pages long.

CHAPTER 7

Create a Great Market Plan

*Prior planning prevents
poor performance*

MARKET PLANNING is a guide to implementation and control. Marketing plan fills out marketing strategy. A market strategy sets a target market and a marketing mix. So, a marketing plan is written statement of marketing, strategy and the time related details for carrying out the strategy.

Thus, the marketing plan should spell out: What marketing mix will be offered; to whom (the target market) and for how long? What company resources will be needed at what rate, the plan should also include some control procedures after the marketing plan is developed, and a marketing manager knows what needs to be done. The marketing manager is concerned with implementation -putting marketing plans into operation; control is simply analyzing and correcting what you have done.

All business strategy is marketing strategy. Your ability to attract qualified prospects determines your success in business. This means that you are responsible for making developing profitable marketing strategies. A market strategy specifies a target market and a related marketing mix. A target market is fairly homogeneous (Similar) group of customers to whom a company wishes to appeal. A market mix is the controllable variables the critical strategic decisions for your business.

Additionally, Market Strategic Planning means finding attractive opportunities and company puts together to satisfy this target group (Product, Price, Promotion and Place).

The effective use of the marketing goals within the marketing mix is an interrelated manner and is the key to successful marketing and tom profitable business. Therefore, the aim of marketing management is to get quality to the right place at the right price, using the right promotional methods.

Your competition determines your level of sales, the prices you charge and how much money you make. Your decisions in these areas determine the success or failure of your business.

This leads to four key marketing principles: specialization, differentiation, segmentation and concentration: -

- **Specialization:** This is the product, service, customer, market, area of technology where you focus all your efforts.
- **Differentiation:** This is your competitive advantage, your area of excellence and superiority, your unique selling position.
- **Segmentation:** You will need to find out who are those customers who most appreciate your area of superiority.
- **Concentration:** This where you focus best possible ways to contact your ideal customers. You also need to decide on the best media and what the most powerful appeals are. A great Marketing plan therefore attracts a steady stream of qualified prospects. Market plan emphasizes your unique selling position and positions your product as the first best choice in the customer's mind.
- **Strategy Preeminence:** Your goal is to position yourself in your market as the only choice for what you sell. The marketing plan thus will help your business define and specify marketing efforts to maximize marketing resources and to increase revenue. You need to customize the marketing strategy, marketing budget, direct competitors, barriers to market entry and more. By investing a few minutes in this chapter, your business will have a thorough marketing plan that will hone marketing efforts and maximize revenue.

ELEMENTS OF GOOD MARKETING PLAN

A. Situation Analysis
  a) External Environment
     i. Regulatory
     ii. Political

      iii. Economic

      iv. Social

      v. International

B. Corporate Review

      i. Mission Statement, Corporate vision, Strategic intent.

      ii. Corporate plan

      iii. Long term goals

      iv. Objectives such as profit, ROI, share price

      v. Organizational Chart

C. Product Category Review

      i. General description (life cycle state, needs/ wants specified)

      ii. Sales trends (years, seasonality, share of major brands)

      iii. Distribution Profile

      iv. Pricing overview

      v. Packaging overview

D. Competitive Analysis

    a) Description of major competitors' strength /weakness

      i. Product

      ii. Distribution

      iii. Pricing

    b) Brand positioning and advertising

      i. Media spending (by medium, seasonality)

      ii. Sales promotion (trade vs. consumer)

      iii. Anticipated major programs (brands, new territories, changes in distribution, pricing, marketing communication)

E. Consumer analysis

      i. Customers/ buyers vs. consumers/ users (& influences)

      ii. Demographics and psychographics

      iii. Purchase rate

      iv. Brand loyalty analysis

      v. Difference between brand and category users.

F. Brand review
G. Current positioning, sales trade, performance test results, awareness, pricing history, distribution history, marketing communication history, stage in brand life cycle, source of additional business.
H. PROBLEMS AND OPPORTUNITIES
    a) SWOT
        i.   Internal Strength and Weaknesses
        ii. External Threats and Opportunities
    b) Opportunity Analysis
    c) Problems

I. STRATEGIC PLANNING: THE BASIC DECISIONS
    a) Marketing objectives (sales: share)
    b) Marketing Strategies
    c) Targeting and Segmenting
    d) Identification or competitive advantage
    e) Positioning and Branding

J. MARKETING MIX OBJECTIVES, STRATEGIES AND TACTICS
    a) Product
        i.   Objectives (new or improved brand/line extension, improvements, deletions)
    b) Place (distribution)
        i.   Objectives (penetration, type outlets, geography, service level)
        ii. Channels
        iii. Warehousing
        iv. Retailing
    c) Pricing
        i.   Objectives
    d) Promotion (communication)
        i.   Personal selling
        ii. Advertising
        iii. Sales promotion
        iv. Packaging
        v.   Direct marketing

K. CONTROL AND EVALUATION
   a) Forecasting
   b) Budgeting
   c) Scheduling and Timing
   d) Evaluation

CHAPTER 8

Attract and Return Great People

> *Right human capital gives competitive edge over rivals*

THE PRACTICE OF HUMAN RESOURCE MANAGEMENT RESOURCE MANAGEMENT (HRM) is concerned with all aspects of how people are employed and managed in organizations. It covers activities such as strategic HRM, human capital management, corporate social responsibility, knowledge management, organization management, resourcing (human resource planning, recruitment and selection and talent management), performance management, learning and development, reward management, employee relations, Healthy and safety and Provision of employee services.

Stone (2010) defines Human Resource Management as a productive use of people to achieve strategic business objectives and satisfy individual employee needs. According to Armstrong (2009) Human Resource Management is a strategic, integrated and coherent approach to the employment, development and wellbeing of the people working in organizations.

Your success in business will be determined by the people who will work for you more than any other factor. It is worth to note that the best businesses have the best people. Success requires excellent performance of each team member, Great people are excellent at their work, they accept high levels of responsibility, they have a positive mental attitude, and they use their time very well and get along with others.

Your ability to find and hire the right and great people is the key to leveraging and multiplying yourself. At this level think through results expected, skills required, personally attributes necessary, write out the job description, cast a wide net, look for achievement history, sense of urgency, intelligent questions, check resumes and references personally, hire slow, fire fast and start them off right and strong.

The concept of hiring and retention n are two sides of the same coin. They complement each other, and if both are done well, they produce what every business desperately needs: first-class human assets. Retention is the converse of turnover – the turnover being the sum of voluntary and involuntary separations between an employee and his or her business. Retention isn't simply a "feel good" issue.

The retention of good employees matters for three important bottom-line resources:

1. The growing importance of intellectual capital:
2. A casual link between employee turnover; and
3. The high cost of employee turnover. What makes retention so challenging is that it is complicated by a number of factors: demographics conditions; cultural expectations and upheavals in the world of work.

Retention is especially challenging when the work force is highly diverse. This is the type of work force that managers in many parts of the world today face. Businesses can best improve their retention rates by crafting creative, specialized strategies for each major segment of the work force.

Every great business has a distribution of low, average and high performers. Nevertheless, most corporate retention programs-which are typically expensive to implement -don't differentiate between them. At the same time every business is subject to labor market forces over which it has little or no control. There is likely to be a "buyer's market "for some job categories and a "seller market" for others. Thus, a company must do its best to identify which employees -or employee's agents represent the highest value to the organization and then apply its resources in a manner that optimizes their retention in a free labor market place.

On one hand one of the realities of market-wise retention is that you will never be able to keep all employees – particularly the most talented, who have the greatest mobility. People retire. They are "poached" by rival, companies. More than a few entrepreneurial types go into business for themselves. Others simply find opportunities that your business can not much. Some businesses create employee turnover as a matter of policy. In the end the struggle to retain good employees is a losing game. Either by death, retirement, defection, everyone eventually leaves. The most you can hope for is to have some influence over who leaves and when.

On the other hand, comes hiring of former employees. Thomas Wolfes message that you can't go home again does not hold true for former employees. Just because a valued person has left your company, don't assume that he or she is gone for good. Some women drop out while their children are infants but are ready to return a few years later. Others leave for what appear to be a great career move, only to be disappointed and disillusioned.

Rehires can a valuable asset for a company. First, they know your business and how to get things done there. This gives them a huge advantage over people hired from the outside, who generally need many months to learn the ropes and become effective. Second rehires return with broader experience and, in many cases, new skills. Finally, every returning defector sends a loud and clear message to others that the grass isn't greener elsewhere.

PART II

HOW TO GROW A SUCCESSFUL GREAT BUSINESS

Chapter 9

Decide on Business Finance: Equity or Debt

If you want to get rich quickly you are on your way to poverty at fast pace

IN FINANCIAL REPORTING, we are normally deal with financial statements that an organization's accounting system produces including the profit and loss account also commonly called income statement, balance sheet and cash flow statements. The income statement presents the financial performance; the balance sheet presents the financial position while cash flow represents the financial adaptability. Out of the three financial statements the balance sheet which represents assets, capital and liabilities shows how the business is financed.

Show Me the Money

Finding the funds to start your business is usually one of the most challenging things the budding entrepreneur will face. Whether yours is a small, home based business or a large venture that requires six or seven figure funding, the good news is that money is available. The bad news is that it is sometimes harder to secure than you may anticipate. But look around. Every one of those businesses that you see as you drive down the street began as someone's dream and somehow, those entrepreneurs found the money to open their doors. If they did, so can you.

New businesses normally have difficult time securing money for a variety of reasons. Conventional financing may be difficult because a new business is a risk to banks-there is no track record or assets to go on. For this reason, almost 75 percent of all start up businesses is funded through other means. In this chapter, those other options are examined.

Money and the New Business

The very first thing required of you is to accurately estimate the amount of money you need. Taking a cold, hard look at your money requirements will help you know your business better and help ensure your success. Once you know how much capital your business will require, it will be incumbent on you to get it. Having a cash crunch from the start is a sure way to go out of business fast. Moreover, a realistic budget will help convince a lender or investor that you understand your business and are worth the risk. The first thing any investor will want to know is how much money will need and how you plan to spend it. They will want specific details on how the money will be spent and how you plan to repay the money.

How Much Money Do You Need?

If you have created a business plan, you should have a pretty good idea how much money you will need to get started. If you haven't figured it out yet, this section will help you. The money you will need can be divided into three categories: one-time costs, working capital and ongoing costs. One-time cost are things that you will need to spend the money on to star your business but will unlikely see again, such as: Legal and accounting costs. You may need to hire a lawyer to help you negotiate contracts, incorporate or perform other legal services. n accountant may be needed to set up your books.

Working capital is the money you will need to keep your business going until you start to make a profit. The old adage "it takes money to make money" is true and real. It is critical to have enough working capital on hand to cover the following costs: Debt payments. If you will be borrowing money to get started, you will want to begin repaying it right away. Inventory and replacement inventory. Service businesses have little, if any inventory, but retail and wholesale companies often spend large sums in this area.

Business finance therefore deals with deciding the capital structure. Capital structure explains how the business is financed. Businesses are either financed either by equity capital or debt capital. These are the main sources of finance. However, each of these has cost of acquisitioning the funds. Thus, if funds are acquired from equity holders the business will pay cost of equity to its shareholders and it funds have been acquired from lenders of finance such as banks the business pays cost of debt normally this is an interest.

Although debt is a way of financing a business in many cases the financial institutions such as banks do not provide the funds to a newly established business because normally banks do not provide the funds to a newly established business because normally banks look for financial statement or collateral of which the business might not have because it is just starting with equity funds.

Since they are two options for financing the business: equity or debt you can also decide to obtain the funds from both equity holders (your own funds) and the banks at the same time. Therefore, in most cases, a company's funds may be viewed as a pool of resource that is combination of different funds with different costs. Under such circumstances it might seem appropriate to use an average cost of capital for investment approval.

Weighted average cost of capital is the average cost of company's finance (equity, debentures, bank loans etc.) weighted according to the proportion each element bears to the total pool of capital. Weighting is usually based on market valuations, current yields and cost after tax. However, the quotion is that higher level of borrowing increases the financial risk and there this must be avoided.

CHAPTER 10

Become a Great Leader

LEADERSHIP is the most important factor for business success. If your vision or dream of starting and growing a great business is to become true you need to engage deliberate efforts of becoming a great leader. Leadership is the ability to get results and thus why leaders must have a clear vision. When I discovered this, leadership became one of my passions.

I love to be a student of leadership and I enjoy teaching it in different forums such as ministry, universities, conferences, seminars and workshops. Leadership is a gift. John Maxwell says for those who are not naturally gifted at its leadership can be mastery. For them leading people is like walking down a dark corridor. They have a sense of where they want to be but they can't see a head and they don't know where the problems and pitfalls are going to lie. For many people in an academic world, leadership is a theoretical exercise an equation n whose variables are worthy of research, study and rigorous debate.

Leadership is a process, not a position. There is a time when people used the term leadership and management interchangeably. I think most people now recognize that there is significance between the two. Management is at its best when things stay the same. Leadership deals with people and their dynamics, which are continually changing. The challenge of leadership is to create change and facilitate growth. Those conditions require movement, which as you will soon see, is inherent in moving up from one level of leadership to another to the next.

Responsibilities of leadership include setting and achieving business goals, market and innovation-continually seek faster, better, cheaper, easier ways to create and keep customers, setting priorities and work on key tasks, focusing and concentrating where superior results are possible, solving problems and make decisions, leading by example, performing and getting results.

This requires points of intensity to discover what decisions and actions you should take to have the greatest impact on other people and your future. Critical thinking in leadership is ultimate. For example, as a great leader in business you need to think of the key result areas and what can you and only you do which, if done well, can make a real difference.

The subject of leadership can be overwhelming and confusing. Where does leadership start? What should we do first? What processes should we use? How can we develop a productive team? How do we help followers become leaders in their own right? The 5 levels of leadership advocated by John Maxwell gives answers to these questions using understandable steps.

Level 1: Position

People follow you because they have to position to the lowest level of leadership- entry level. The only influence a position leader has is that which comes with a job title. Position leadership is based on rights granted by the position and titles. Nothing is wrong with having leadership position. Everything is wrong with using position to get people to follow you. Position is poor substitute of influence.

People who may take it only to level one may be bosses, but they are never leaders. They have subordinates, not team members. They rely on rules, regulations, policies and organization charts to control their people. Their people will only follow them within the stated boundaries of their authority. And their people will only do what is required of them. When the position leaders ask for extra efforts or time, they rarely get it. Position is the only level that does not require ability and effort to achieve. Anyone can be appointed to a position.

Level 2: Permission

Level 2 is based entirely on relationships. on the permission level, people follow because they want to. When you like people ad treat them as individuals who have value, you begin n to develop influence with them. You develop trust. The environment becomes much more positive -whether at home, on the job, at play or while volunteering.

The agenda for leaders on level 2 isn't preserving their position. It's getting to know their people figuring out how to get along with them.

Leaders find out who their people are. Followers find out who their leaders are. People build solid, lasting relationship. You can like people without leading them but you cannot lead people well without leading them but you cannot lead people without liking them. Thus, what level 2 is about.

Level 3: Production

People follow you because of what you have done for the organization. One of the dangers of getting to the permission level is that leaders may be tempted to stop there. But good leaders don't just create a pleasant working environment. They get things done! Thus why they must move to level 3, which is based on results. On production level, leaders gain influence and credibility and people begin to follow them because of what they have done for the organization. Many positive things begin to happen when leaders get to level 3. Work gets done, morale improves, profits go up, turnover goes down and goals are achieved. It is also on level 3 that momentum kicks in.

Leading and influencing others becomes fun on this level. Success and productivity have been known to solve a lot of problems. On level 3, leaders can become change agents. They can tackle tough problems and face thorny issues. They can make the difficult decisions that will make a difference. They can take their people to another level of effectiveness.

Level 4: People Developnment

People follow you because of what you have done for them. Leaders become great not because of their power but because of their ability to empower others. This is what leaders do on Level 4. They use their position, relationships and productivity to invest in their followers and develop them until those followers become leaders in their own right. The result is production: Level 4 leaders reproduce themselves.

Production may win games, but people development win champions. Two things always happen on Level 4. First, team work goes to every high level because the investment in people deepens relationships, helps people to know one another better and strengthens loyalty. Second, performance increases relationships, helps people to know one another better and strengthens loyalty. Second, performance increases because there are more leaders on team and they help to improve everybody's performance. Thus level 4 leaders change the lives of people they lead and the people follow them because of that. Their relations are often lifelong.

Level 5: Pinnacle

People follow you because of who you are and what you present. The highest and the most difficult level of leadership is the Pinnacle. While most difficult level of leadership is the pinnacle. While most people can learn to climb to Level 1 through 4, Level 5 requires not only effort, skill and internationality but also a high level of talent. Only naturally gifted leaders ever make it to this highest level. Level 5 leaders develop people to become Level 4 leaders. Developing leaders to the point where they are able and willing to develop other leaders is the most difficult leadership task of all. But they are pay offs: Level 5 leaders develop Level 5 organizations. They create opportunities that other leaders don't. Their leadership gains a positive reputation. They create legacy in what they do. As a result, Level 5 leaders often transcend their position, their organization and sometimes their industry.

Insights on Leading from the levels; If you want to become an effective great leader and lead the way successful people that run great businesses do, then you must master the 5 Levels of leadership. Here are some insights that will help you to understand how the levels relate to one another. You move p a level but you never leave the previous one behind. You are not on the same level with everyone. The higher you go, the more time and commitment is required to win a level. Moving up occurs slowly, but going down can happen quickly. The higher you go, the greater the return. Moving further up always requires further growth. Not climbing the levels limits you and your people. When you change positions or organizations, you seldom stay at the same level. Lastly, you cannot climb the levels alone.

CHAPTER 11

Successful Advertising Strategies

Not Advertising is like being alone in a dark room. You know you are there, but no one else does

The whole idea of almost all advertising is to turn on the light and let people know you are there. You have to get the phone to ring or get people to come in the store. Advertising will do that.

Advertising Options

Advertising in the newspaper is a great, inexpensive way to reach a big audience. Newspaper ads can be used to promote a sale, grab attention, or offer specials on your product or service. The downside is that newspapers carry lots of ads, so yours can get lost.

Magazine ads cost more than those in the paper, but magazines stay in the house longer than a newspaper, so the price may be worth it. Magazines are especially good for promoting your image and building your brand. Trade magazines are useful for business to business advertising.

Radio can be an expensive, a high impact way to reach a specific market. Repetition is essential with radio advertising as studies show that it often takes someone hearing your ad six times before it sinks in.

Television advertising is very effective, but is correspondingly expensive. Car companies know more about how to sell their product than almost anyone, and where do they advertise most?. Television advertising works, bottom line. Cable channels are more affordable, but are seen by far fewer people.

Yellow pages advertising are not cheap, but it delivers people who are ready to buy now. Internet advertising is not expensive, but not all that effective in many cases either.

Outdoor advertising offers high visibility, and the cost per viewer is relatively low.

Let's look at each of these advertising options in more detail.

Internet:

Internet billboard ads were once the rage, but not today. While industry execs swear by them, to most people, they are an annoyance to be clicked off as soon as possible. You had better be quite sure someone is going to read your internet ad before dropping your money here.

Outdoor:

Outdoor ads, billboards, bus stop ads, and transit ads can be a good way to attract attention and get the phone to ring because they can be seen by hundreds of thousands of people each month. According to Market Vision Research, the Florida Lottery found that the most effective way to advertise its product was through the use of billboards.

Creating a Winning Ad

No matter which option you choose, you still need to create an ad that pulls. Interestingly, all ads, no matter the media, are fairly similar in structure. They all must grab attention and make an offer. One simple way to create a successful ad, whatever the media is through the tried and true AIDA method. This stands for attention, interest, desire and action. The AIDA formula serves as a good blue print for creating a winning ad of any type -newspaper, magazine, radio or television.

Attention

The first thing you have to do is grab their attention. Once you do that, you can get a potential customer interested in what you are selling.

If you don't get their attention. Once you do that, you can get a potential customer interested in what you are selling. If you don't get their attention, they will not receive your message among the distractions of the headline news, sports stories and other more distinctive ads. You must first hit your prospect between the eyes with a powerful headline. A good headline will grab a customer by the throat, show them the benefit of hearing more, and do so in two or three seconds.

When writing your ad, keep in mind the benefits that are most likely to get attention include saving money, saving time, making money and better health. Beyond the headline, another way to capture their attention is to use a great visual or photograph. One's eye is naturally drawn to pictures, so incorporating one into your headline can really make a difference.

Interest and Desire

After you have the prospects attention, you have to make your pitch in the body of the ad. You do that by making the customer a compelling offer and describing as many benefits as possible in simple and interesting terms. Because the product or service must fill a market need to be successful, you must explain how it does that. Your ad must e well written so it clearly explains the benefits to customers and keeps their attention.

Action

Finally, you must ask for the order. Give reason for the customer to buy now, and make it easy for him or her to do so. This will involve a coupon for mail orders, a toll-free order line, an email address, an online order form, a fax order line, or any other means to make it easy and simple to order. Be sure to take the fear out of the purchase as much as possible by giving guarantees, offering testimonials and showing how the customer is going to miss out if he doesn't order NOW! If you follow the AIDA formula, you should find that your ad works, no matter what the medium.

CHAPTER 12

Successful Marketing Strategies

CUSTOMERS DO NOT APPEAR out of nowhere. They must hear of your business before they will ever call you, and that is the purpose of marketing. What is marketing? Essentially, it is anything you do to promote your business, get your name remembered, and generate sales. It encompasses promotions, giveaways, publicity, customer relations, public speaking, signs-anything that keeps your business in the public eye and brings customers in the door.

The Need for a Marketing Plan

The lawyer's tale above is illustrative because it indicates just how few people really have a comprehensive, methodical, well-thought-out plan for generating sales. And make no mistake about it, whether you are opening a dentist's office, a real estate agency, or a bakery you will be in sales.

How are you going to generate those sales? In which media sources will you advertise and which marketing options will you utilize? A marketing plan will tell you. A marketing plan is nothing more than your plan of action for bringing in business. It need not be long or complicated, it simply needs to be a blueprint that you believe will for you and to which you are committed.

Your assignment for the rest of this chapter is to look at the various marketing tools available to you, decide on a few that make sense for you and your business, and commit those to paper, along with any advertising strategies you have decided on. Committing to a marketing and advertising plan of action will keep you focused and on target.

Correspondence

Any marketing campaign begins with your letterhead, stationery, business cards etc. These seemingly insignificant things are actually quite important because they represent you to the outside world. If your letterhead is professional, then you are seen as professional. Use high quality paper, include all information, including email and fax numbers. All correspondence must be coordinated. Your fax cover sheet should mirror the letter head which should mirror your business car.

Newsletters

Physical and virtual newsletters are a great way to share information with both potential and actual clients. Aside from positioning you as an expert, they are inexpensive to create and allow you to contact people without looking like a salesperson.

Tap into the magic words. The two greatest words ever invented for business are FREE! And SALE! People love to get something for less, almost as much as they love to get something for less, almost as much as they love to get something for less, almost as much as they love to get something for nothing. If you utilize these two words in your promotion, marketing and advertising materials, people are sure to notice you.

Contests

A contest can generate interest and free publicity for your business.

Signs

A big, bold sign in the right location can be a very effective way to bring in new business. Retail businesses swear by good signage. A number of different factors need to e considered when choosing a sign:
- From what distance do you want the sign to be seen?
- Do you want it to be seen at night?
- What kind of weather will it be exposed to?
- How much can you afford to spend / Shop around?

- Can you legally put up the sign you desire? Check the zoning ordinances in your area. If your proposed sign is illegal, you will first need to get a variance from the city.

Telemarketing

You can buy some very specific lists and hire inexpensive telemarketers, even students, to sell your product or services over the phone.

Telemarketing can also be used to let current customers know of a sale or other promotion.

Direct Mail

Like telemarketers, direct mail merchants can also generate some very specific lists, which you can use to send potential customers a flyer or other info. Direct mail is also a great way to stay in touch with current and former customers and is less impersonal than telemarketing. Here are some tips for making direct mail effective.

Define your Audience

The more specifically you can define who your potential customer is, the more successful your direct mail campaign will be.

Commission salespeople

Another way to increase business is by having commissioned salespeople sell your wares to different retail stores. The obvious advantage here is that you don't have to pay the salesperson anything until he or she gets a sale and even then, payment will come from the proceeds of the sale.

Brochures

When you go into a car showroom to look at a new car, what do you leave with? A brochure. The reason is that a brochure enables a potential customer to practically take your product with them and review it at home.

Magnets

All refrigerators are covered with pictures and magnets these days. If you want people to see the name of your business several times a day, give away free refrigerator magnets. This idea works especially well for neighborhood services and restaurants.

Web

Website can be a great marketing tool. You can put your site address on all of your stationery, so people can check your site out later. Aside from sites. Even if you are not planning an e-commerce business, having a promotional your own Website, consider the possibility of expanding your business by selling your wares on eBay or other online malls. I once did a bankruptcy for an antiques dealer.

Two years later, I ran into him at the airport. He told me he was on his twice-yearly trip to Europe. Apparently, after the bankruptcy, he began to sell his antiques on eBay and his business just took off.

Excellence

It costs five times more to create a new client than to retain an existing one. Studies show that each satisfied customer will spread the good word about your business to at least one other person, while an unhappy customer will likely complain to many more than that. Doing great work and offering superior customer service can go a long way toward creating continuing revenue.

Publicity and Public Relations

Another important aspect of marketing is the ability to get good press for your company. A newspaper article or television news story about your business is like a commercial and an endorsement all in one. Even better: You can copy the article or make tapes of the story and use them later in other promotions.

Newspaper editors and television producers have to come up with stories to fill their pages and airwaves -day after day, week after week-and it is not always easy to fill all that space. Therefore, your business, along with your ability to publicize it properly and work cooperatively with the media can become one of the stories if you do it right. So just how do you get the press to pay attention to your business? Begin by reading the paper or watching your local news closely and noticing which reporters do stories about small businesses.

Then you need to think of a "hook" or angle for the story. Local boy makes good is but one example. If your sponsor a charity event, invent something new, lead your community, or open a new store in a needy neighborhood, the press might just become interested in your story. Come up with a hook. There are two ways to get a media outlet to pay attention to you: sending out a press release or sending out a press kit. A press release is a one- or two-page article that explains the who, what, where, when and how of your "news". If an editor or producer agrees that the contents of the press release are indeed newsworthy, they will either assign a reporter to interview you about the story or possibly just print the press release outright in the paper. A typical press release may read something like the following.

Chapter 13

Buying Franchise and other Businesses

One of the best ways to start a new business, if you do it right, is to buy franchise or other established business. While people typically think of Mc-Donald's, KFC, Dunkin Donuts or Baskin Robbins when they think of franchises, the fact is that franchises come in almost every industry and take a lot of the risk out of the entrepreneurship equation.

FRANCHISES

Franchising is a method of distributing services or products. With a franchise system, the franchisor (the company selling the franchise) offers its trademark and business system to the buyer, or franchisee who pays a fee for the right to do business under the franchisor's name using the franchisor's methods. The franchisee is given instructions on how to run the business as the franchisor does using the franchisor's name and the franchisor supports the franchisee with expertise, training, advertising and a proven system.

Buying into a proven system is important. The franchises that work best are those where the franchisors have worked out the kinks and translated its business into a systematic procedure that the franchisee follows. Do what the franchisor did, and you should get the results that it got; that's the idea. As franchisors are won't to say, when you buy a franchise, you are in business for yourself but not by yourself.

The reason that a franchise can be a smart business decision is that in the right franchise system, the franchisor has already made the mistake so you don't have to. Franchising should reduce your risk. You need not reinvent the wheel. In exchange for its expertise, training and help, however, you will be required to give up some independence and do things the franchisor's way.

Finding the Right Franchise

With so many franchise systems from which to choose, the options can be dizzying. It is best to start with a global perspective. In the universe of franchising, which industries seem to match your interests? Narrow the choices down to a few industries in which you are most interested and then analyze your geographic area to see if there is a market for that type of business.

Once you have decided which industry interests you most and seems to have growth potential in your area, contact all the franchise companies in that field and ask them for information. Any reputable company will be happy to send you information at no cost. A great place to learn about all of your options is at a franchise trade show. This is a terrific way to gather a lot of preliminary information and survey the field in a short period of time and you can find them in most good-sized cities.

When attending a franchise trade show, keep a few thoughts in mind. First remember the companies exhibiting at the show by no means make up all of the franchise opportunities available. Indeed, these events showcase only small selection of the available franchise programs.

Analyzing the Franchisor

As you go about this research, understand that successful franchisors have certain traits in common. Following are the traits that are most important. If you can find a franchisor that has these traits, you are headed in the right direction.

The Franchisor Supports the Franchisees

The best franchises are ones where the franchisor sees its relationship with the franchisees as a partnership. As Steve Reinemund, the former Head of Pizza Hut, puts it, "Franchisees are only as successful as the parent company is only as successful as the franchisees". Not only do such exceptional franchisors offer plenty of communication, opportunities for growth within the company and help during hard times they also offer lots of advice and training.

A good example of this is Dunkin' Donuts. To support new franchisees, it created Dunkin' Donuts University. There, franchisees and their personnel are invited to attend a six-week success program that teaches them everything from basic instructions on how to run the business to how to produce the products, deal with employees, and use equipment. It even offers advice on inventory control and accounting. Now that's support.

The Franchisor is Committed to Customer Service

The great franchisors don't just give lip service to customer service. They teach it to everyone in the organization and live it on a daily basis. That's critical because if people are treated well at other outlets, that, in turn, gives your individual franchise a good name too. As the Pizza Hut chairman put it, "We are committed to more than just good service we are committed to providing legendary service."

The Franchisor Changes with The Times

Tastes and values change. The last thing you want is to buy into a system that is stuck in the past, not realizing that its product o service needs to adapt to the times. The better franchise systems are constantly test marketing new ideas and new products in an effort to stay ahead of the competition. Typically, a good franchisor will provide the following services on an ongoing basis:

- Local, regional and national advertising, offering you related programs and materials
- Field support
- Updates to the operating manual and ongoing related training for you and your management team
- Some sort of advisory council
- Research and development of new products, services and system enhancements
- Communication support-either an intranet, a member only Website, monthly newsletters or some other method to keep you up to date. If the franchisor you are considering does not offer these sorts of things, it would behoove you to think twice.

Location, Location, Location

Not all franchises nee to pick a dynamite location. For example, janitorial services, direct mail companies, or lawn care services really don't need to worry about their location because drop-in business is not their business model. But a restaurant needs a good location. Typically, if you are looking at a retail establishment, location usually is a priority.

The first thing to do is speak with a potential franchisor. One of the best aspects of buying into a good franchise operation is that you should get plenty of advice and help from the franchisor. Start there and see what it says. The franchisor, will know what you should look for, what works best and what locations are available the franchisor will be helping you in the site selection process. Additionally, you need to find out about territorial exclusivity.

Does the franchisor offer this and if so, what is the size of the territory? Territorial exclusivity has been the subject of many lawsuits between franchisees and franchisors, so make sure that you really understand this issue and have any agreements put in writing. As always, one of the best ways to know what to expect from a franchisor on this or any subject is to talk to the current franchisees. They will tell you if the franchisor plays fair, if territorial limits are respected, and if site location analysis is accurate.

Area Development

A topic related to location n is area development. Area development allows you to open more than one franchise in a certain locale. If, for example, you want to open and buy the rights to your area en masse. This allows you to monopolize the market and excludes challengers under the same franchise umbrella from competing with you. The key things to consider regarding area development are; -

- Picking a franchise system that is not yet developed in the area.
- Getting the franchisor to grant you market exclusivity.

Avoid Common Mistakes

Once all of your questions have been satisfactorily answered, you have done your due diligence and have spoken with existing franchisees and you understand where you store will be allocated, it is time to sign on the dotted line. But before you do, make sure you avoid potential pitfalls. Franchises often buy into a franchise without a full understanding of just what it takes to succeed in their chosen business. That is one of the several common mistakes that are easily avoidable.

CHAPTER 14

Caring for Customers and Employees

Advertising and marketing have the same goal in mind; to make the phone ring or bring customers in the door. After that, what happens is up to you. If customers like what they see, if they find great products or services, if they are treated well, they will return. When that happens, you have the most prized of all things: a valued, loyal, returning customer. According to Inc. magazine, it costs five times more to create a new customer than it does to retain a current one. Similarly, there is a rule that says that 80 percent of your business comes from 20 percent of your customers (the 80/20 rule).

The best thing you can do to stay successful in business is to make new customers, consistent customers by treating them well, giving them exceptional service and doing what you say you will do when you say you will do it. By the same token, you also need to care for your employees. Employees are the backbone of your business. If they are happy, your business runs well; if they are not, well, you know. Your job once you get your business up and running (among your many other jobs) is to care for these two constituencies. Take care of your customers and employees, and they will care of you.

The Three Stages of Customers

Almost every business will have three different types of customers: new customers, existing customers and exiting customers. You need to know how to handle all three correctly if you want to succeed in business. Creating new customers is an ongoing process, and it is one of the fun aspects of business. Many entrepreneurs enjoy spending their time figuring out ways to lure in business. Where many drop the ball, however, is after the initial sale. Flush with success, a new entrepreneur often neglects the new customer after that sale, inadvertently failing to realize that the new customer may become one of the valued 20 percent if treated properly.

You turn that new customer into a returning customer by treating him or her well from the start. If you don't, it's the business equivalent of non-night stand. Existing customers are one of your most valuable business assets and cannot be taken for granted. They usually make up the bulk of your business, so it is incumbent upon you to nurture that relationship and let those customers know how important they are Existing customers should be given special services and discounts when appropriate and should always be shown appreciation for their patronage.

Finally, all business will have customers who are ending their relationship for one reason or another and even this customer needs special treatment. The ending may just be the natural course of the relationship; for example, a chiropractic patient who is ending his care or customer who is moving away. Because you never know who they talk to or who they may refer to you, this customer needs to be cared for just as well as the others.

What is Great Customer Service?

While "great customer service" is a mantra we all hear about, few businesses actually incorporate it into their modus operandi. It may be because they have never given it much thought, or because they have never given it much thought, or because it is simply not a priority, or that the culture of the company may be so hectic that employees feel stressed.

Unless you want to be on a never-ending quest for new customers because you have no returning, loyal ones, you had better make customer service a priority. Furthermore, serving your customers well is also a great way to distinguish your business from the competition. You have to give people a reason to patronize your business-better prices, a better location, better products or yes better service. The essence of superb customer service is that a service becomes one of the guiding principles of your business.

You need to put pen to paper, create a policy and then see that every employee receives and understands it. Also, make sure that it is made a part of the employee manual. For employees to realize how important you take customer service, it must be stressed every day, in many ways.

Great Customer Service

Be attentive. Think like a customer. What do they want from you? What are their needs? The better you can meet those needs, the better your customer service. Make it personal. Endeavor generally to anticipate the needs of particularly special customers. Offer recommendation and ideas that they might be able to use. Become their partner. Send them a handwritten thank you or other token of your appreciation. They won't forget it. Give them a discount. A discount on future purchases is a great way to make customers feel special (and remain loyal).

Keep them informed. Costco sends its all-important small business customers as special newsletter every month loaded with information, business tips, ads and discounts. Can you do something similar?

Take personal responsibility. Make sure customer service representatives act promptly, keep their promises and follow up. The idea is to have one person accept responsibility for fixing a problem, do more than a client expect and do so in a positive, helpful way.

Go the extra mile. Infusing your troops with the power to solve basic customer problems without seeking extra authority will not only increase the level of your customer service, but it will simultaneously show your employees how important customer service is to the company.

A. Hard work and perseverance
B. Fine products and service
C. Advertising
D. Knowing the fundamentals of business
E. Employees

The overwhelming answer was E, employees. It is not hard to understand why. Employees do the work. Employees make decisions. Employees are on the front lines. It follows then that if you want to offer great customer service, you have to infuse your employees with that desire, because for many businesses, it is the frontline employees who deal with customers on a daily basis. If you want to be known for having great customer relations, your staff needs to know what is expected of them.

Helping Your Employees Help Your Customers

Support employees who deal with customers every day. Make their jobs easier. If they have what they need, they will be happier and that will translate to the customer. Waiters at Outback Steakhouse, for example, are allowed to offer patrons free food after a problem has arisen.

Train all employees in customer service. One CEO takes training so seriously that he often teaches the customer service class given to new hires himself. This training should also include phone courtesy training, which is the first contact many people have with your business. Stress communication. Again, those who deal with customer complaints need to know how to solve the problem and need to tell the customer that they will solve it.

Make sure they keep the customer up to date and offer a solution in a timely manner. Reward a job well done. Have "no tolerance" policy. Never tolerate employees who give poor customer service, no matter how bright they maybe. If you begin to stress the importance of increasing the quality of your customer relations and back it up with actions, the message will be received. Poll customers frequently to get feedback on how you're doing not only do most customers not mind giving feedback, they feel important when they do. Stress manners. Customers like hearing "Thanks you" or "We're so sorry" or other considerate words, when appropriate.

Handling Complaints

Indeed, feedback from your customers, whether positive or negative, is one of the most valuable things your business can get. According to the SBA, most business owners get one to five complaints a week and most are about billing and pricing. Interestingly, the SBA survey also says 95 percent of dissatisfied customers would do business again with a company if their problems were quickly and satisfactorily. Solving the customer's problem is your job, even if you disagree with his or her complaint.

All you need to do is listen. To win back dissatisfied customers, be willing to hear them out instead of being defensive. Then placate angry customers by letting them know you are more than happy to correct the problem to their satisfaction. After listening: Ask the customer how he or she would prefer the problem be resolved and resolve it that way if you can. If a customer wants a refund, give it to him or her, if possible. If you do, you will likely keep a customer.

If the problem has to do with employees, discover whether the problem is endemic and, If so, root it out. Even if are convinced that your business I not to blame, be humble, express your regret that the customer had a bad experience with your company and offer something to mollify him or her. Complaints are good because they help you learn what your business is doing wrong. But feedback need not be negative to be helpful.

Soliciting feedback is a valuable way to find out what customers like and dislike about your business, as well as a way to discover what they would change or keep. By offering a small gift certificate for participating, you can learn a lot of valuable information from your clients, while also getting their addresses that you can add to your mailing list. Another benefit of using customer feedback surveys is that you get testimonials from them. Once you get their permission, those testimonials can be used in your marketing and promotional materials. Customer feedback can be one of the best friends your business has.

Caring for Employees

Not only must your customers know they are appreciated, but so should your employees. There are many ways you can run your business. You can be a dictator, a jerk, a facilitator, a cheerleader, or any number of other personalities. The important thing to realize is that the style you choose to use will, in large part, determine the kind of business you create. If your employees learn to loathe you, you can bet it will affect the bottom line, just as it would if they learn to love you.

A trait common to many highly successful businesses is that the owners and managers put a lot of effort into communicating with employees to make sure they are happy and motivated. A simple but highly effective thing you can do to create a positive work environment is to be, like Ronaldo Reagan, a great communicator. Good communication could be a quarterly "state of the company" report to employees, encouraging them to give suggestions or ask questions, or it could be one-on-one meetings devoted to career goals. Another thing you can do to create a great work environment is to be sure to properly reward your great work environment is to be sure to properly reward your employees.

A large part of making employees happiness has to do with compensation. Compensation comes in many forms, the most obvious of which are paychecks, bonuses, profit sharing and stock options. While the thought of sharing profits with employees may nausea to you, consider that doing so becomes an incentive for them to do well, it improves productivity and shows your appreciation for a job well done.

Less evident rewards can also make a difference too. A gift certificate, a luncheon to honor employees who have made outstanding contributions or free T-shirts all help boost morale. "Share your profits with all your Associates and treat them as partners. In turn, they will treat you as a partner, and together you will all perform beyond your wildest expectation. Remain a corporation and retain control if you like, but behave as a servant leader in a partnership. Encourage your Associates to hold a stake in the company. Offer discounted stock, and grant them stock for their retirement. It's the single best thing we ever did"-Sam Walton, Made in America.

There are many measures for employee's satisfaction beyond money. Employees want to be appreciated and they want a life outside the office. Knowing that happy employees create a happy workplace and usually a more productive and profitable workplace, it is not a bad idea to take the pulse of your staff once or twice a year to see how you are doing. The things that you want to find out, via a feedback form, private meeting or some other method, include:

- If the employee fees that he is cared about as a person, not just a cog in the machine
- If the employee feels her work is appreciated and praised
- If he feels that people care what he has to say
- If she likes her job and what she would change about it.
- What he needs to perform his job better (tools, training, equipment, supported, etc.)

You will be spending a lot of time t your new business and with your employees. Being a good boss is one of the easiest and least expensive, ways to ensure the success of your business.

The Mission Statement

Another way to let employees know what is expected of them is to create a mission statement for your business. A mission statement is a very effective business it tells you, your employees and your customers just what your business is really about and where it is supposed to be headed. Knowing what your mission is also helps you know whether your daily activities and policies, are getting you closer to or further from your goal. Thus, it not only keeps you focused; it also helps employees understand what is expected of them.

Many small businesses have a mission statement prominently displayed somewhere and employees often pay it lip service. But great businesses get their employees to actually buy into that mission and believe in it. When employees don't understand what the business is about, or if they are forced to heed to some maxim that they neither buy into nor believe is true, morale suffers. Conversely when they feel part of something larger, their value increases.

Creating a Mission Statement

Your mission can be either personal or for your business. In this exercise, we will create one for your business. It should be between 50 and 400 words. It is your dream, your focus, your purpose. Create a mission statement by answering the following questions:

- What personal values do you want to be embodied in your business?
- What qualities and characteristics should be best exemplified by your business?
- What resources are at your disposal?
- What is your niche?

- What is your grand vision for your business? (Don't be shy!)
- Based on your values, vision, characteristics and resources, what is the purpose of your business?
- Which of your personal qualities do you want to be infused in the business?
- How can your business best serve your clients, family, employee and investors?
- How much money do you want to make? What are your markets? Who are your customers?
- What is your responsibility and commitment to them?
- Are you willing to commit to your mission, your vision, your dream? Are you willing to pay the price, whatever that is? Based on your answers above, based on your values, dreams, plans, niche, resources, etc.,

Draft a mission statement for your business. Make it large and bold and fantastic: something you believe in all of your heart. Surrender to your purpose. One anonymous writer explains the value of a mission this way: "By intentionally raising your own expectations of yourself, you create a gap between where you are and where you choose to be. Having created this gap for yourself, everything about you automatically begins working on your behalf to close it. This explains why people with a mission enjoy boundless energy."

Here's is an example: Mission Statements can also be created in conjunction with your employees. The value f doing this is that everyone owns the result. The downside is that you may not like the result. For a new start-up, it is probably best to have the top management create the mission statement, and then help all new employees buy into from the day they are hired.

Liven Up Your Meetings

The purpose of a meeting is to share information, brainstorm and work toward accomplishing a goal. But that's not what happens at most meetings and employees tend to tune out when and meetings are confusing, lack focus or are boring. Bad meetings result in more meetings, lower morale and decreased productivity.

It need not be so. These tips should produce both better meetings and thus a more efficient business:

Keep it short and sweet. Meetings run into trouble when they are allowed to continue and nauseam. Of course, some meetings need to be long, but those should be exception. Most meetings, if they stick to a well-thought-out agenda, can be finished in well under an hour and good facilitator should keep the meeting on track and moving forward.

Speak plain English. Jargon and mumbo Jumbo waste time and make the meeting pointless.

Offer recognition. Recognize the winners on your team. Take a few minutes to congratulate and thank them for meeting goals, closing deals and making money. Praise reinforces positive behavior and encourages everyone to do well.

Open up your circle. Bring in people from the real world. Have a customer attend a sales or staff meeting and explain why he or she buys from you. This is a powerful dose of reality.

Take action. It is good idea to create an action plan at the end of every meeting. The plan will list each task that needs to get done, who will do it, and when it will be completed. The action plan should be distributed to everyone who attended. If your meeting becomes a way to help your staff make more money instead of a rote rendition of the last meeting, then you just might find that the once-dreaded sales or staff meeting is no longer an unwelcome chore.

CHAPTER 15

Hard to Copy Strategies

Fortune Favours the brave

What is a Strategy?

ONE CAN TAKE A CHARACTERISTICS APPROACH in order to define what this is. A strategy is usually concerned with long term direction of a business. Strategic decisions are likely to be concerned with the scope of organization (s) activities e.g. what should the organization's core business be for instance? Here scope of work becomes very fundamental to the strategy. This is because it concerns the way in which those responsible as managers conceive the organization's boundaries.

Strategic decisions aim at achieving some advantage for the organization over competition. Strategy can be as a search for strategic fit. With the business environment. This could men major resource shifts or changes in an organization's e.g. decision to reposition one in the market. Strategy also creates opportunities by building on an organization's resources and competences. This is called the resource-based view of strategy.

This is concerned with exploiting the strategic capability of an organization in terms of resources and competencies. The idea is to provide a competitive advantage and yield new opportunities. Examples include small organization changing its focus in order to suit its capabilities. The strategy of an organization is affected not only be the environment and forces and strategic capability. Also, by the values and expectations of those who have power in around the organization n.

From the foregoing strategy s the direction and scope of n organization over the long term which achieves advantage in a changing environment through its configuration of resources and competences with the objective of fulfilling stakeholder expectations. Strategy is the game plan management is using to stake out a market position, conduct it operations, attract and please customers.

Among the most important strategic decisions are those relating to growth, especially how to grow a business. It is tempting to believe that continuing to do what has been done in the past will lead to continued growth. If managers are to make the right decisions, therefore, a strategic direction and set of guiding priorities are needed together with an assessment of the most effective strategy for growth.

Levels of Strategy

Strategies exist at a number of levels in an organization. We distinguish three levels of strategy: Corporate, business and functional or operational level. While strategy may be about competing and surviving as a firm, one can argue that products, not corporations compete and products are developed by business units. The role of the corporation then it is to manage its business units. The role of the corporation then is to manage its business units and products so that each is competitive and so that each contributes to corporate purposes.

On the other hand, while the corporation must manage its portfolio of businesses to grow and survive, the success of a diversified firm depends upon its ability to manage each of its product lines.

1. Corporate Level Strategy

This is concerned with overall purpose and scope of a business organization and how value will be added to the different parts (business units) of the organization. This could include issues of geographical coverage: diversity of products, service or business units, resource allocation between different parts of the organization. Basically, corporate level strategy fundamentally is concerned with selection of business in which the company should compete and with the development and coordination of that portfolio of businesses.

What is clear is that corporations are responsible for creating value through their businesses. They do so by managing their portfolio of businesses are successful over the long-term, developing business units and sometimes ensuring that each business is compliable with others in the portfolio.

2. Business Level Strategy

Business level strategy is about how to compete successfully in particular markets. This concerns which products or services and markets should be developed. How can advantage over competitors be achieved in order to achieve organization goals and objectives. It could be long term profitability or market share growth. Whereas corporate strategy level involves decisions here need to be related to strategic business units.

A strategic business unit is part of an organization for which there is a distinct external market for goods and services that is different from another Strategic Business Unit (SBU). These can be conceptualized in geographical terms structured around regional business units. Hence, they become the primary foci for business level strategy. These would change in the scope and type of customers and products.

3. Operation or Functional Level Strategy

This can b described as the third level strategy. These are strategies concerned with how the component parts of an organization deliver effectively the corporate and business level strategies in terms of processes and people. In most businesses successful businesses depend to a large extent on decisions that are taken on activities that occur at the operational level. The integration of operational decisions and strategy is therefore of great importance as mentioned earlier.

Therefore, simply put functional level strategy of a business organization is the level of operating divisions and departments. The strategic issues at the functional level are related to business processes and the value of the firm.

Strategic Capability

This is made up of resources and competencies. You can think about this by considering strengths and weaknesses (whether its is a competitive advantage /disadvantage). The aim is to form a view of the internal influences and constraints on strategic choices for the future. It is usually what we call core competencies, a combination of resources and high levels of competence that provide advantages with competitors find difficult to imitate.

Strategic Formulation

In crafting a strategy management is saying, in effect "among all the paths and actions we could have chosen, we have decided to move in this direction, focus on these markets and customer needs, compete in this fashion, allocate our resources and energies in these ways and rely on these particular approaches to doing business."

A strategy thus entails managerial choices among alternatives and signals organizational commitment to specific markets, competitive approaches and ways of operating. Closely related to the concept of strategy is the concept of a company's business model. This a term now widely applied to management's plan for making money in a particular business. More formally, a company's business model deals with the revenue cost-profit economics of its strategy.

The task of strategy is to make business more valuable. This means moving it from A to B and guiding people clearly on how to make this journey. The development of business strategy involves three distinct phases: analysis, planning and implementation.

Analysis

When analyzing a business's strategy there is no constantly right answers, but there are some constantly right questions. As the business and business environment change, the best answers will change over time. The solution is to question rigorously, decide the best approach and then check the course of action through further questioning. A successful external analysis process should not be an end in itself. Rather, it should be motivated throughout by a desire to effect strategy, to generate or evaluate strategic options.

The investment decision, where to compete, involves questions such as: should existing business areas be liquidated, milked, maintained or invested for growth? What growth directions should receive investment? Should there be market penetration, product expansion, should new business areas be entered? The areas that require the analysis, competitor analysis, market analysis, industry analysis, portfolio analysis and environmental analysis. There is often a tendency to relegate the external analysis to annual exercise.

The annual planning cycle can provide a stimulus to review and change strategies that can be health. However, a substantial risk exists in maintaining external analysis as once-a year event. Thus, the need for strategic review and change is often continuous. Information sensing and analysis therefore need to be continuous. External analysis deliberately commences with customer and competitor analysis.

Planning

Marketing management also involves using the information gained from market analysis using the information gained from the market analysis to plan the organization's marketing response/activities.

Control

The third main component of marketing management is to control the operationalization of the marketing plan. Control involves setting measurable targets for the plan and then checking performance against these targets. If necessary remedial action will need to be taken to ensure that planned and actual performances are brought into line.

CHAPTER 16

Business Growth Strategies

> **If things are not affecting
> your thinking, then they are
> not affecting your life**

THE DIFFERENT ROUTES to growth are as follows:

Organic Growth

This occurs when a business grows by using its exist existing resources. Organic growth can take place because the marketing is growing, or because the business organization is doing increasingly better than its competitors or is entering new markets. Exploiting a product advantage can sustain organic growth. Organic growth depends on a firm's available resources and capabilities as well as its planning, time and cash.

Mergers and Acquisitions

One of the fastest routes to growth is through an acquisition or merger, but it is one of the hardest and riskiest. There are two views about mergers. One is that mergers between titans will result ion an even larger titan, too cumbersome to operate as flexibility and efficiently as it needs to. According to this view a merger results in more bureaucracy, diminishing returns negating the benefits of increase in size and capacity for production, diseconomies of scale, swallowing huge quantities of capital and causing organizational lethargy; and a lumbering giant that will be outpaced and outsmarted by smaller rivals.

The second, more optimistic, view is that mergers result in: economies of scale and efficiency; stability and greater potential for growth resulting from a broader base of customers and products; and an intellectual capital and management infrastructure to deal with market change.

Specialization

The opposite of diversification, specialization involves dropping non-core activities, or even redefining and focusing on core operations. The main advantage are clear focus and strength in depth, with all available resources channeled into one endeavor. It also means that any cash available from the sale of non-core operations can be used to grow on the business. Reliance on specialization requires doing what you do sufficiently better than your competitors and successfully anticipating and adapting to market changes.

Competitive Advantage

When a firm sustains profit that exist the average of its industry, the firm is said to possess a competitive advantage over its rivals. The goal of much of business strategy is to achieve a sustainable competitive advantage. Michael Porter identified two basic types of competitive advantage: cost advantage and differentiation. A competitive advantage exists when the firm is able to deliver the same benefits s competitors but at a lowest cost (cost advantage), or deliver benefits that exceed those of competing products (differentiation advantage). Thus, a competitive advantage enables the firm to create superior value for its customers and superior profits for itself.

Cost and differentiation advantages are known as position advantages since they describe the firm's position in the industry as a leader in either cost or differentiation. A resource-based view emphasizes that a firm utilizes its resources and capabilities to create a competitive advantage that ultimately results in superior value creation.

Segmentation Strategy

What is market segmentation? Is a relatively homogenous group of customers who will respond to a marketing mix in a similar way. Market segmentation is a two-way process: naming broad product markets and segmenting those broad markets in order to select target markets and develop suitable marketing mixes. A good market segmentation should have the following characteristics: homogeneous (similar) customers in a segment should be as similar as possible with respect to their likely responses, heterogeneous (different) customers in different segments should be as similar as possible with respect to their likely responses, substantial- the segmenting dimensions should be useful for identifying customers and deciding on marketing mix variables. Reasons for segmenting include: to understand the customers, to focus activities, to reduce risks, to defeat the competitors and to assist in planning.

There are three ways to develop market-oriented strategies in a broad product market. The single target market approach-segmenting the market and picking one of the homogeneous segments as the firm's target market. The single target market approach -segmenting the market and picking one of the homogeneous segments as the firms target market, the multiple target approach-segmenting the market and choosing two or more segments then treating each as a separate target market needing a different market mix and the combined target approach -combining two or more submarkets into one larger market as a basis for one strategy.

All these three approaches involve target marketing. (1) And (2) are called segmenters and (3) are called combiners. They try to develop a different marketing mix for each segment. Segmenters usually adjust their market mixes for each target market. Segmenters believe that aiming at one or some of these smaller targets makes it possible to satisfy the target customers better and provide greater profit potential for the firm. These include geographical, behavioral and demographic characteristics, qualifying dimensions are those relevant to including a customer type in a product market.

While determining dimensions include those that actually affect the customer's purchase of a specific product or brand in a market. Cluster analysis and positioning are a more sophisticated computer aided technique of segmenting the market. It involves finding similar patterns within sets of data. Focusing on target market helps one to find tune the marketing mix.

Positioning

This is another approach which helps identify product market opportunities. Positioning shows how customers locate proposed or present brands in market. It entails some formal marketing research. Managers should decide whether to leave the product (and marketing mix) alone or reposition it e.g. an advert. This may mean physical changes in the product or simply image changes based on promotion. Firms often use promotion to help "position" how a product meets a target market's specific needs. Positioning helps managers understand how customers see their market. This is called "Perpetual mapping".

BCG Growth-Share Matrix

Businesses that are big enough to be organized into strategic business units face the challenge of allocating resources among those units. Boston Consulting Company Group developed a model for managing a portfolio of different business units (or major product lines).

Experience Growth

The premises of the BCG findings are these: That in any market segment of an industry price level tend to be very similar for products. Therefore what makes one company more profitable than the rest must be the levels of its costs. It is the key determinants of low cost levels that the BCG attempted to unearth. Their arguments can be summarized as follows:

Total Units Produced

The relationship between unit costs and total costs produced overtime. Significant cost is a function of experience and then cost is a function of a market share. Market share does not necessary relate to the overall market. The overall implications of BCG's findings are that successful companies make almost all their profits from products in which they dominate their market segment. This view has become very strong influence on many company's choices of strategy.

Product Portfolio

In order to dominate a market a company must normally gain that dominance when the market is in growth stage of the product lifecycle. In a state of maturity a market is likely to be stable with customer loyalties fairly fixed. It is therefore more difficult to gain share. The BCG has suggested the model of the product portfolio or the growth share matrix as a tool by which to consider product strategy. The matrix combines market growth rate and market share and thus directly relates to the idea of the experience curve.

The BCG growth- share matrix displays the various business units on a graph of the market rate vs. market share relative to competitors:

HIGH (Market Share) LOW

HIGH	Stars	Question Marks
(Market Growth)	Cash Cow	Dog
LOW		

Fig 16:1 *BCG Growth- Share Matrix*

Resources are allocated to business units according to where they are situated as follows:

A question mark (or problem child) is in a growing market but does not have a high market share in a growing market but does not have a high market share. Its parent company may be spending heavily to increase the market share.

A star is a product (or business) which has a high market share in a growing market. The business is able to break even and make profits though it spends heavily to increase the market share.

A cash cow is a product (or business) with high market share in a mature market. Because growth is low and market conditions are more stable the need for heavy marketing investment is less. The cash cow is thus a cash provider.

Dogs have a low market share and low market growth. They are cash drain. To portray alternative corporate growth strategies, Igor Ansoff presented a matrix that focused on the firm's present and potential product and markets (customers). By considering ways to grow via existing products and new products, there are four possible product-market combinations.

Fig 16:2 Ansoff Matrix

	EXISTING PRODUCTS	**NEW PRODUCTS**
EXISTING MARKETS	Market penetration	Product development
NEW MARKETS	Market development	Diversification

Market Penetration- the firm seeks to achieve growth with existing products in the current market segments, aiming to increase its market share.

Market development- the firm seeks growth by targeting its existing products to new market segments.

Product Development- the firm develops new products targeted to its existing market segments.

Diversification- the firm grows into new businesses by developing new products for new markets.

Resource Based View Strategy

Organizations are dynamic entities, linking the activities through a set of connections that can be both complex and simple. Emphasizing one aspect or resource in the business has profound implications for the rest of the organization. Understanding how to assess and manage this web of interactions lies at the heart of systems thinking and is central developing a flexible and robust strategy and then implementing it successfully. Kim Warren, a management writer, highlights the fact that possibly the greatest challenge facing managers is to understand how to build their businesses' performance over both the short and long term.

When the causes of performance through time are not understood companies tend to make poor choices about their future. They embark upon plans they cannot achieve, failing to assemble what they need. This is called critical path the journey the business takes in seeking to improve its performance and value.

Strategic Position

Influences of expectations on an organization's purposes are and corporate governance is crucial in strategic positioning important. For instance who should the organization serve/ how should managers is held responsible. Note that the expectations of various stakeholders also affect purposes. Who prevails depends on who has the greatest power. Cultural influences from within the organization and around the world also influence the strategy and organization.

Strategic Choices

Strategic Choice involves understanding the underlying bases for future strategy at both the business and corporate levels and the options for developing strategy in both the directions in which strategy might move and methods of development. There are strategic choices in terms of how the organization seeks to compete at business level.

This involves the identification of a basis for competitive advantage. This arises from an understanding of the markets, customers and strategic capability of the organization. At the highest level there are issues of corporate level strategy. These are concerned with the scope of an organization's strategies. It includes decisions about portfolio of products and or business and spread of markets. For most organizations international strategy are a key apart of corporate level strategy.

Parenting is part of this strategy. It involves the relationship between separate parts of the business and how the corporate parent adds value to these parts e.g. exploring synergies within an organization can add value.

Strategy Implementation

Translating strategy into action is concerned with ensuring that strategies are working in practice. Structuring an organization to support performance includes organizational structures, processes and relationships and the interaction between these. Enabling success through the way in which separate resources of an organization support strategies.

Managing strategy involves change most often and how the context of an organization should influence the approach to change depends on different types of roles for people managing change.

Integrating the Strategy

The strategy needs to take account of the realities of the business. To succeed, it must be consistent with the work of the other departments, the capabilities of employees and suppliers and the expectations of customers. The challenge is to avoid confusion or conflict.

Communicating

Clear communication is crucial in developing and implementing a strategy, but communication skills are often overlooked and leaders frequently forget they can always be improved to benefit the organization and everyone within it.

ENTREPRENEURIAL STRATEGIES

Entry Strategies

Routamma (1999:20) point out that entrepreneurial wedge be grouped into five entry strategies: developing a new product or service: creating parallel competition by Developing a new product or service; buying a Franchise; finding sponsorship; and acquiring.

Developing a New Product or Service

What it takes a company around a new product or service includes, most importantly, the discover of an intersection between the market for that product or service and away to create one.

Creating Parallel competition by Developing New Product or Service parallel completion often fierce. By definition it involves firms that lack strong differentiation and therefore tend to compete on price, which drives margin down. The toughness of such competition will likely force the entrepreneur to be good at performing the function of the business.

Finding Sponsorship

A safer best as an entry wedge may be taken to advantage of the willingness of someone to help sponsor the startup in some manner. Typically the sponsor is a customer, a supplier or an investor in the startup venture. A prime requisite for all these type of sponsorship is that the sponsor as credible and likely to succeed regard entrepreneur and venture the venture. The strongest basis for this is usually a track record of prior accomplishment and a demonstration that the entrepreneur possesses the capacity to perform the critical task of the venture.

Acquiring a Going Concern

The final main entry strategy is to acquire a going concern. This can simplify the process of getting into business can be viewed as basically bundle of habits-customers buying, suppliers supplying, employees doing their jobs. In a going concern, those habits are already present.

Expertise in a going concern should already be present in employees of the business. Even if it is not, the buying entrepreneur should be able to obtain education and operating help from the selling owner to fill in the expertise needed. Consequently, it is fairly common to find business owned by entrepreneurs who bought them with no prior experience in that particular line of business and nevertheless succeeded.

Strategies for managing Industry Competition

Doyle (2002) observes that the slow economic growth rates that have characterized many industries in recent years have given way to zero-sum markets. A company can therefore only grow by beating others. Thos calls for a strong competitor's strategy. Aaker (2001) states that maintenance of a strong market position or the achievement of rapid growth usually reflects a strong market position or the achievement of rapid growth usually reflects a strong and success competitor strategy. The converse this statement is that rapid decline and weakening of business positions reflects a poor competitor strategy. Whether this is true for the case of SME's in Malawi is open to argument.

D'Aven (2002) argues that when established companies do succumb to a revolution, they usually have only themselves to blame. Either they have ignored the threat for too long. Or they have hyperactively embraced it too quickly, wasting their resources and destroying their existing strengths without acquiring new ones.

These arguments stipulate that a careful understanding of the right response to competitor activity as well as achieving the business objective of long-term survival, growth and profitability. This literature on competition strategies insights into the business competitive environment and deserves lessons for achieving improved performance through employment of successful competitor strategies.

Wilson (1999) observes that increasingly, competition is not between individual companies, but rather between whole networks-with the prize going to the company that has built better network. The operating principle is simple: build a good network of relationships with key stakeholders and profits will follow. Christopher (2001) puts more emphasis to this school of bought by stating that in today's market, "supply chain now competes against another supply chain" (Christopher, 2001, pp 22).

This calls for competing players in a market to look beyond their direct competitors and start search for strategic competitive advantages across the whole range of the supply chain in which they are involved.

CHAPTER 17

Business Portfolio

When you have excellent results, in your field people will listen to you

A PORTIFOLIO is the collection of different investments that make up an investor's total holding. A portfolio management might be the investments in stocks and shares of an investor or the investments in capital projects of a company. A portfolio might be the investments in capital projects of a company. Portfolio theory, which originates from the work of Markowitz, is concerned with establishing guidelines for building up a portfolio of stocks and shares, or a portfolio o stocks and shares, or a portfolio of projects.

The same theory applies to both stock market investors and to companies with capital projects to invest in:-

- **Security:** Maintenance of capital value
- **Liquidity:** If made with short term funds, should be convertible into cash with short notice.
- **Return:** Obtain highest return compatible safety.
- **Spreading risks:** Spread risks over several investments, so losses on some offset by gains on others.
- **Growth prospects:** Investment in steadily growing businesses.

The risk in investment, or in a portfolio of investments, is the risk that the actual return will not be the same as expected return. The actual return may be the higher, but it may be lower.

A prudent investor will want to avoid too much risk, and will hope that the actual returns from his are much the same as what he expected them to be. The risk of security, and the risk of portfolio, can be measured as the standard deviation of expected returns, given estimated probabilities of actual returns.

The risk of an investment might be high or low, depending on the nature of the investment. Low risk investments usually give low returns. High risk investments might give high returns, but with more risk of disappointing results. So how does holding a portfolio of investments affect expected returns and investment risk?

CORRELATION OF INVESTMENTS

Portfolio theory states that individual investments cannot be viewed simply in terms of their risk and return. The relationship between the return from one investment and the return from other investments is just as important. The relationship between investments can be one of three types.

Positive Correlation

When there is positive correlation between investments, if one investment does well it is likely that the other will do well. Thus, if you buy shares in one company making umbrella and in another which sells raincoats you would expect both companies to do badly in dry weather.

Negative Correlation

If one investment does well the other will do badly, vice versa. Thus if you hold shares in one company making umbrellas and in another which sells ice cream, the weather will affect companies differently.

No Correlation

The performance of one investment will be independent of how the other performs. If you hold shares in a mining company and in a leisure company, it is likely that there would be no relationship between profits and returns from each. This relationship between the returns from different investment is measured by the correlation coefficient. A figure close to +1 indicates high positive correlation, and a figure close to -1 indicates high negative correlation, then by combining them in a portfolio overall risk would be reduced. Risk will also be reduced by combining in a portfolio investment which has no significant correlation.

As well as being measured correlation, the relationship between returns on two investments can be measured by covariance. The covariance is an absolute measure, whereas the correlation coefficient is a relative measure, varying as we have seen, between, between -1 and +1. A positive covariance indicates that the returns will move in the same direction.

PORTFOLIO THEORY AND FINANCIAL MANAGEMENT

Our discussion of portfolio theory has concentrated mainly on portfolios of stocks and shares. Investors can reduce their investment risk by diversifying, but what about individual companies choosing a range of businesses or projects to invest in?

Just as an investor can reduce the risk of variable returns by diversifying into a portfolio of different securities, a company can reduce its own risk and so stabilize its profitability if it invests in a portfolio of different projects or operations, assuming that any positive correlation between returns is weak.

Should Companies try to diversify?

Diversification may have the following advantages for shareholders. Internal cash flows will become less volatile. This makes it less risky to service the company's current level of debt and may consequently allow the company to make use of more debt without additional risk. This could reduce the cost of capital generally, increasing the wealth of shareholders.

Diversification into foreign markets may enable shareholders to reduce the level of their systematic risk where exchange controls or other barriers to direct investment exist. The diversifying company can enable this to occur by investing in markets which have a combination of risk and return which shareholders would not otherwise be able to obtain.

A diversified company may have a lower probability of corporate failure because of the reduced total risk for the company. This will reduce the likely impact of insolvency costs. However, there are a number of reasons why a company should not try to diversify too far.

A company may employ people with particular skills, and it will get the best out of its employees by allowing them to stick to doing what they are good at. A manager with expert knowledge of the electronics business, for example, might not be any good at managing a retailing business. Some managers can adapt successfully to running a diversified business. When companies try to grow, they will often find the best opportunities to make extra profits in industries or markets with which they are familiar.

If a market opens up for say, a new electronic consumer product, the companies which are likely to exploit the market most profitably are those which already have experience in producing electronic consumer products. Conglomerates are vulnerable to take over bids where the buyer plans to 'unbundle' the companies in a group and sell off individually at a profit, particularly because their returns will often be mediocre rather than high, and so the stock market will value the shares on fairly low P/E ratio.

Separate companies within the group would be valued according to their individual performance and prospects, often at P/E ratios that are much higher than for the conglomerate as a whole. Except where restrictions apply to directly investment.

Limitations of Portfolio analysis

Portfolio analysis is useful for diversifying through firm's investment decisions. Applied to the selection of investment proposals, portfolio theory has a number of limitations. Probabilities of different outcomes must be estimated; fairly easy for (e.g.) machine replacement, more difficult for (e.g.) new product development. Shareholders preferences between risk and return may be difficult to know and personal tax issues may impact. Portfolio theory is based on the idea of managers assessing the relevant probabilities and deciding the combination of activities for the business. Managers have their job security to consider, while the shareholder can easily buy and sell securities.

Managers may therefore be more risk averse than shareholders, and this may distort managers investment decisions (the agency problem) Projects may be of such a size that they are not easy to divide in accordance with recommended diversification principles.

The theory assumes that there are constant returns to scale in other words that the percentage returns provided by a project are the same however much is invested in it. In practice, there may be economies of scale to be gained from making a larger investment in a single project. Other aspects of risk not covered by the theory may need to be considered, e.g. bankruptcy costs.

International Portfolio Diversification

Approximately 7% of total world equities have been estimated to comprise cross-border holdings. Even so, it is arguable that there remains a domestic bias among many types of investor, which can be attributed to a number of barriers to international investment, including the following: Legal restrictions exist in some markets, limiting ownership of securities by investors.

Foreign exchange regulations may prohibit international investment or make it more expensive. Double taxation of income from foreign investment may deter investors. These are likely to be higher information and transaction costs associated with investing in foreign securities. Some types of investor may have a parochial home bias for domestic investment. There are a number of arguments in favor of international portfolio diversification.

Diversification of Risk

A portfolio which is diversified internationally should be less risky than a purely domestic portfolio. This is of advantage to any risk-averse investor. As with a purely domestic portfolio, the extent to which risk is reduced by international diversification will depend upon the degree of correlation between individual securities in the portfolio.

The lower the degree of correlation between returns on the securities, the more risk can be avoided by diversification. On the international dimension, a number of factors help to ensure that there is often low correlation between countries and therefore enhance the potential of risk reduction, including the following: Different countries are often at different stages of the trade cycle at any one time. Monetary fiscal and exchange rate policies differ internationally. Different countries have different endowments of natural resources and different industrial bases. Potentially risky political events are likely to be localized within particular securities markets in different countries differ considerably in the combination of risk and return which they offer.

PART III

EXPLOITS IN BUSINESS

CHAPTER 18

Wealth Creation

Remember the Lord your God who gives you power to get wealth

THE REAL FACT is that we all want to be well off, wealthy, rich and abundant. And we are fascinated by others who already are. The question is how did they do it? How can we do it too? The simple truth is that wealth people tend to understand and do things the rest of us don't. From mindsets to casual actions, they follow behavioral when it comes to their wealthy and these rules are what separate them from everybody else. This chapter codifies what those behaviors are so that you too can choose to be more wealth. The basis of the rules is that these are the things I have observed wealthy people do. This means that if we do like them, we will become like them. This actually does work.

Wealth creation involves knowing to do to make money, how to carry on making money, how to hang on once you have got, how to spend, invest and enjoy money and make use of it altruistically. This assumes that you want to get richer, do it legally, do something useful with it once you have got it, put something back, keep some of this stuff under your hat and that you are prepared to put a bit of work.

"He becometh poor that dealeth with a slack hand: but the hand of the diligent maketh rich"

Proverbs 10:4

Therefore this chapter is about thinking wealth, getting wealth, staying wealth and sharing your wealth. We start with thinking wealth because that's the foundation on which all things wealth related rest.

Proverbs 23:7 says: **For as he thinketh in his heart so is he ...**

Wealthy Thinking

Money is a concept. You can't really see or touch it. You can only do that with some physical symbol of it like bank notes or cheque. Bits of paper yes but bits of paper with enormous power. The good news about becoming wealth is that anybody can make money that anybody can make money and that this is not selective or discriminatory. You have the same rights and opportunities as everyone else to take as much as they take. What else could make sense? There is no way money can know who is handling it, what qualifications are, what ambitions they have or what class they belong to. It is very clear that money has no ears or eyes or senses ears. Money is there to be used, spent, saved and invested, fought over, seduced with and worked for it.

Knowledge

Everything you know or believe about money did not come to you at birth. You were conditioned in your attitude towards finance as you grew in your family or environment of your upbringing. Until the knowledge you have of finance is appropriate one for wealthy creation, every plan you have gets messed up by the disjointed opinions you hold. Every time you want to create wealthy you might find at the back of your mind things rising against it thus causing you make excuses and reject what finances are coming your way.

So thinking that money is scarce, evil bad or dirty to come to you until you get the right education. Robert Kioyosak author of Rich Dad and Poor Dad says there are three forms of education: academic, professional and financial education. People are not wealth and even go to the extent of being poor because they are financially illiterate. To be financially mis-educated is to use slow words like "I will never be rich". Financial mis-education will teach you to write strong business proposals that will create jobs for others and profit for companies and not have to create something for your future.

Multiplying money is a skill and requires that you be adequately informed and continues to inform yourself on how to make money and see it increase. You must ask yourself how you will put your brain to work instead of asking how you can afford things. Wealth creation rests in educating your mind and you need to know that being broke it is a temporary thing but poverty is eternal. You must educate yourself to know that multiplying money is necessary because money is a form of power and once you have it you have the ability to respond.

Dedication

Dedication and commitment is the next step after acquiring financial knowledge. Commitment must be put into action by crafting a game plan. Wealth people would not have become who they are by chance by taking tangible actions.

> **Seest thou a man diligent in his business? He shall stand before kings; he shall not stand before mean men**
> Proverbs 22:29

If you are to leave where you are to where you are ought to there must be clear description of the road map. You have got to have a plan. The plan gives you the important bit-how you are going to get there. This is a function of strategic vision which is a description of the road map. This type of thinking will make you to put your heart and soul into your assignment which will create wealth for you.

Investment

Many business commentators say that investment simply means the science of money making money. This means that once your commitment towards creation is established the next thing is to start the journey in investment. This is important because you cannot become wealthy only by looking wealthy.

Then he who had received the five talents went and traded them and made another five talents.

Matthew 25:16

This is a call to develop the ability multiplying money. With most people, when money gets into their hands, it reduces in quantity. But with some, it multiplies when it reaches their hands. Financial success and wealthy is not all about spending money; it is about making money. The major problem is that most of us we were not taught how to make money in schools. Most of our money habits were picked up from our home. We learn how to spend money and not how to make money. The man with five talents he traded with what he was given.

And likewise he who had received two gained two or more also. But he who had received one went and dug in the ground and hid his Lord's money.

Matthew 25:17

This is amazing. If you are in your 20's and 30's and you don't want to be broke at the age of 70, do something now. It is almost too late to start when you turn sixty. Your money habits today determine your financial future. However, financial success is progressive. Until you can manage the hundreds you have, you are not prepared to handle the thousands, then millions and then billions. It is progressive. Until you pass the test on this level, God will not allow you to advance to the next level. He says;

You have been faithful over few things; I will make you rule over many things.

Matthew 25:23

God predicts that what you will do with the millions by what you do with the thousands. Money will always flow away from those who do not know how to treat it well. Different ways to invest include leveraging, treasury bills, investing in stocks, bonds, and general business, mutual trust funds, real estate and investing in financial institutions such as banks.

**So you ought to have deposited my money with the
bankers and at my coming I would have received bank
my own with interest**

Matthew 25:27

That is the minimum, the least. Here we cannot talk about the savings
account. The interest you earn from the savings account is not multiplication.
It is a reduction of your money. By the time you factor in inflation at the end of
one year and add interest on it, you will realize that the rate of inflation is higher
than the interest your money is earning hence you would have lost money in
real terms. From today you will not be on the losing end but prospering side.

How to be Wealthy

Riches require that you have enough money. But wealth goes further.
It is having enough of all the essential of life such as love, good healthy,
friends and family, spiritually and of course, total package-laughter, love,
living, good healthy, peace, money and relationships.

The following are proven ways on how you can become wealthy:
wealthy thinking; developing an understanding of the power of small
and big savings; spending less than you earn; always paying yourself first;
saving something out of each dollar; being responsible for where you are in
life; paying cash and use less credit; buy stocks not product; keeping track
of your money; study and admire the successful in your chosen assignment
or field; recognize the difference between income statement wealthy and
balance sheet wealth; do not confuse between debt and wealthy; invest in
right ground; form new habits which encourage you in the direction of
becoming wealthy for God; set financial goals and assess them; refuse to be
stressed ; make conscious decision to handle your money matters yourself;
create your own entity; become finically literate and give generously.

How to Stay Wealth

To maintain or sustain wealth is a skill and it requires commitment
to the proven wealthy principles. It is a matter of following the rules of the

game. It goes without saying that those that love rules will be rulers and those that love commandments will be in command.

To stay wealth requires you to follow certain rules. Here are the rules: don't spend it before you've got it; put something aside for your old age- no more than that; put something aside for emergencies or rainy days-this is the contingency fund; never lend money to a friend unless you are prepared to write off; find ways to give people money without them feeling they are in your debt and lastly share your wealthy.

Sharing wealthy simply means using wealthy wisely. Those who abuse their wealth wisely. Those who abuse their wealth don't tend to stay wealth for long.

> **That they do good that they be rich in good works ready to distribute willing to communicate**
>
> 1 Timothy 6:18

Sharing wealth is the same as giving. We are not to be mere reservoirs that hold on to the blessings; but those who will pass it for others too to enjoy. When God called Abraham, he said He would bless him to be a blessing to his generation.

> **And I will make of thee a great nation, and I will bless thee, and make thy name great; and thou shalt be a blessing**
>
> Genesis 12:2

The process of giving and receiving is what makes the cycle of life to be perpetuated and be enjoyable. Those that keep to themselves do not increase. There is that scatterth and yet increaseth and there is that with holdeth more than is meet but it tendereth to poverty.

> **The liberal soul shall be made fat and watereth shall be watered also himself**
>
> Proverbs 11:24-25

CHAPTER 19

Let the Figures Make Noise

BUSINESS AND MONEY are practically one in the same. How much should you charge for your goods or services? Should you extend credit? How do you go about accepting credit cards? Whatever the issue, understanding the financial aspect of business vital.

Making a Profit

Just how important is selecting the right price? It could mean the difference between success and failure. One of the most important financial concepts you will need to learn in your new business is the computation of profit and how it relates to your pricing structure. The gross profit on a product sold or service rendered is computed as the money you brought in from the sale, less the cost of the goods sold. The key is to compute accurately the cost of goods sold, which can be deceptive.

Pricing Your Goods or Service

It should be clear by now that the wrong price can put you out of business fast. Finding that magic number requires careful thought and planning. The trick is to come up with a price that gives you a good profit while still attracting customers. When first opening their doors, many business people have a hard time knowing what to charge for their product or service. But actually, it's not that hard to figure out. If you sell a product, you base your retail price on your wholesale cost. The real trick is figuring out what to charge when you have a service business.

Cheaper Isn't Always Better

It is equally important to understand that being the cheapest isn't always smart. When you use price as the only barometer for your services, then other more important things get left out of the equation-like quality, personal service and promptness. McDonald's can emphasize low prices because that is one of its trademarks. But if you are not a McDonald's-type outfit, constantly discounting fees and prices may be a mistake.

The price of a product tells consumers what kind of value and quality to expect before they buy it. A person who can afford a Mercedes or Jaguar doesn't mind the high price because they associate quality and value with the prices of these cars. Often, in a consumer's mind, a higher price, high quality and a low price means poor quality. You need to ask yourself whether you are trying to increase profit margins or market share. If you are mostly interested in boosting profits rapidly.

Let the Figures Do the Talking

If you don't understand the finances of business and many entrepreneurs actually do not, you are in trouble. Business decisions that are not based, at least in part, on a cold and hard financial analysis are decisions that can easily go wrong. For example, assume that your business is looking to add a new product line.

How do you know if it will work? Such an important decision should not be based on guesswork or hunches. Instead you have to let the figures do the talking. Knowing how to crunch the numbers-figuring out what it will cost you to launch the newline, how much you can expect to make, and how quickly you can reasonably expect to make it-will make the decision easy for you.

Can you afford a new product line? Will your cash flow allow you to afford it? What kind of return on this investment of capital and time can you expect? Let the figures do the talking. That's what Starbucks does. How does Starbucks know when to open up another store in a neighborhood? They look at existing stores and notice how long customers have to wait to have their order taken and filled and then open another in that area when the wait gets too long. They let the figures do the talking. That is what you must do.

Can you afford that new product line? Well, what do the numbers say? If the numbers are not there, your brainstorm could be a huge mistake. And if you don't what the numbers are saying, it is time to learn. Supply and demand for the product you are producing. It has to be done with testing and care. The second way to increase your gross profit margin is to lower your costs.

Decreasing the costs of materials or producing the product more efficiently can accomplish this. Look for a less costly supplier. Whether you are starting a service business, a manufacturing outfit, a wholesaling venture or a retail store, you should always strive to deliver your product or service more efficiently, with less cost and at a price that gives you the best profit. The name of the game is, after all, making a profit.

Your Customers Payment Options

The final financial aspect you need to deal with at this point has to deal with at this point has to do with what forms of payment to accept. This includes the creation of a credit policy and the decision of whether to accept checks and credit cards.

Extending Credit

If you do decide to extend credit to customers, be picky. There are two important aspects to a successful customer credit policy. First, limit your risk. Second, investigate each customer's creditworthiness. One a potential customer has completed the application, you need to verify the facts and assess the company's creditworthiness. You do so by calling references and by using a credit reporting agency or a business consulting firms. Finally, even if the client seems worthy, and even if he or she checks out, trust your gut.

CHAPTER 20

Money Management

MONEY MANAGEMENT OR FINANCIAL MANAGEMENT is that branch of management accounting which deals with the management of finances in order to achieve the financial objectives of an organization. It deals with the acquisition and allocation of resources among firms, the firm's present and potential activities and projects. Acquisition is concerned with the "financial decision", the generation of funds internally or externally at the lowest possible cost. Allocation is concerned with "investment decision", the use of these funds to achieve corporate financial objectives.

Corporate Financial Objectives

The conventional assumption is that most trading organization's objective is the maximization of the value of the company for its owners. Since the owners of a company are its shareholders, the primary objective of a trading company is said to be "the maximization of shareholders wealth. The wealth comes from dividends received by the shareholders wealth. The wealth comes from dividends received by the shareholders and the market value of the business, that is, capital gains from increases in market. In achieving this objective, other objectives are suggested due to the existence of other interest groups with stakes in the company including, leaders, employees, the community at large, government etc.

It must be emphasized enough that while companies do have to consider other stakeholders, from a corporate finance perspective, such objectives should only consider other stakeholders, from a corporate finance perspective, such objectives should only be pursued in support of the overriding long term objective of maximizing shareholders wealth. Modern Finance theory usually assumes that the objective of the firm is to maximize the wealth of shareholders.

Other possible objectives of the business include: Maximizing profits Market share, obtaining greater "Managerial Power", Increasing Employee Welfare, Increasing Social Responsibility and Corporate Growth. These objectives are operatives but tend to be less important than maximizing shareholders wealth.

Agency Theory

Large corporations characterized by separation of ownership and control. This may lead to conflicts between management and shareholders. Conflicts may also arise between: Group of bondholders (e.g. subordinated versus unsubordinated + debt) Groups of shareholders, bond holders and shareholders, Management Personnel (scarce corporate resources).

Management Vs Shareholders

It should be clear that the corporation can be viewed as a complicated set of contractual relationships among individuals. It should be noted that, equity is a Residential Claim. As owners of the cooperation the relationship with management is one of Principal- Agent. It is assumed that, left alone managers and shareholders will each attempt to act in their own interest. Thus managers have day to day operational control of the firm. Manager's goal I the maximization of a "Corporate Wealth", in other words the wealth over which management has control. Corporate wealth is not equal to shareholder wealth.

Agency costs

These are costs associated with resolving the conflicts of interest between managers and shareholders e.g. audit costs. There is however a trade – off between the costs and benefits of controlling management. Agency costs also incur when managers do not attempt to maximize film value and shareholders incur costs to monitor the managers and influence action. There are no costs when the shareholders are also managers. Owner manager has no conflict of interest. This is one of the advantages of sole proprietorship.

Financial institutions are financial intermediaries that accept deposits from savers and invest in capital markets. Their functions range from accepting, payment mechanism, borrowing and lending and pooling risks. Classes of these intermediaries include: deposits institutions e.g. banks, insurance companies, trust companies e.g. money managers, credit union and mutual funds. The financial systems within the financial institution include: people (Investors and borrowers), place (market), product (securities e.g. treasury bills). Price (costs of capital and cost of borrowing or simply interest.

Capital markets

Capital markets or financial markets as there are commonly called are markets that manage the surplus units and deficit unit e.g. those that have money will invest in the capital/ financial market. Similarly those that do not have will go and borrow from these markets.

Objectives of the capital markets include: providing link between companies raising funds for their expansion and people with funds to invest. Providing a market place for buying and selling of shares at market determined price3. Supervising trading activities so as to ensure that the interests of customers are looked after and are carried out fairly properly according to the governing rules of exchange.

Treasury Functions

Treasury management is the corporate handling of all financial matters, the generation of internal and external funds of the business, the management of currencies and cash flow and complex strategies, policies and procedures of corporate finance. Liquid management making sure that the firm has liquid funds it needs. Funding management concerned with all forms of borrowing and alternative sources of funds such as leasing and factoring, bank loans, debentures, etc.

Currency management exposures policies and procedures. e.g.

international monetary economics. Corporate finance, equity, capital management business acquisition and sales and project finance. Maintaining relationship with banks, stock holders and other investors who hold the firms securities.

Centralized cash management has some advantages. For example it avoids having a mix of cash surpluses and overdrafts in different localized bank account. Larger volumes of cash are available to invest giving better short term opportunities. e.g. treasury bills. Any borrowing can be arranged in bulk at lower interest rates than for smaller borrowings. So too the decentralized cash management has advantages: sources of finance can be diversified and can match local assets. Greater autonomy can be given to subsidiaries and is more responsive to the need of individuals operating units.

Costs of funds

When you get a loan from a bank, the bank charges interest on the loan. The interest that you get is the cost of lending the money. In other words, the bank could put the money to other use and earn profit equivalent to or more than the interest that you pay on the loan. Cost of funds or the minimum required return a company should make on its own investment to earn the cash flows of which investors can be paid their return. Therefore cost of capital is the minimum acceptable return on an investment.

Cost of funds has three elements. First, the risk free-rate – this is the return one would get if a security was completely free of any risk. Second, risk free yields are typically o government securities, for example yields on Treasury Bills and third, the premium for business risk – this is an increase in the required rate return due to compensate for existence of uncertainty about the future of a business.

Costs of funds can be cost of equity or cost of debt. Cost of equity could be estimated by dividend valuation model, which is based on the fundamental analysis theory. This theory states that the market value share is directly related to expect future dividends on the shares. The cost of debt capita already issued is the rate of interest (the internal rate of return), which equates the current market price with the discounted future cash receipts from the security.

Weighted average cost of capital

In most cases, a company's funds may be viewed as a pool of resources, that is, a combination of different funds with different costs. Under such circumstances it might seem appropriate to use an average cost of capital for investment approval. High level of debt creates financial risk. Financial risk is measured by gearing ratio.

$$\frac{D}{E + D}$$

Higher gearing will increase KE (cost of equity) where D stands for debt and E stands for equity. As level of gearing increase the cost of debt remain unchanged up to the certain level of gearing. The Ke (cost of equity) rises as the level of gearing increases (need for high returns). The WACC does not remain constant and then begin to increase as the rising cost of equity/ debt becomes more significant. The optimum level of gearing is where the company's weighted cost of capital is minimized. This assumes that WACC is unchanged coz of the following two factors: cost of debt remain unchanged on the level of gearing increases. Cost of equity rises in such a way to keep the WACC constant.

Cash Flow Forecasting

A business has a responsibility to make payment when they are due regardless of whether sufficient cash has been collected from customers to provide the means of payment. Unpaid supplies may be begrudgingly tolerant and wait a little longer for their cash. But they may refuse to fulfill orders until payment is made and they may even take legal action to recover to debt. This requires the corporation to prepare cash flow statement.

Cash flow statement presents financial adaptability. It is a statement of cash inflows and cash out flows. On one hand key cash inflows include: cash sales, receipts from debtors coming as a function of credit sales: this means the finance department must have a strong credit control section which should intensify on debt collections; sell fixed assets such as vehicles, furniture's, computers and equipment among others and other e.g. donations or grants.

On the other hand cash out flows include: payment of creditors, payment to lenders of finance, Administrative expenses such as salaries, rentals, insurance among others, dividend pay-out, taxation such as corporate tax, purchase of fixed assets such as vehicles, furniture, computers and equipment, investment into projects and other business portfolios. To enable management to plan appropriately and feel confident that payment can be made as they fall due, a detailed cash flow forecast is required that predicts timing and amount of receipts and payment.

The advance warning of any potential cash shortages that are revealed allows management the time to put together a considered rather than active, plan for bridging any gaps in cash flow. It can take time to negotiate with the banks and raise additional finance and with a well-instructed and realistic cash flow forecast this can be done well in advance of any potential need. Furthermore, a well – constructed cash flow forecast helps banks and other providers of finance confidence in management realism and competence.

Table 20:1 A cash flow forecast

	Month 1	Month 2	Month 3	Month 4	Month 5
Opening balance	6,000	5,200	6,400	(1,500)	(2,000)
Receipts	8,300	(12,600)	4,900	8,801	1,600
Payments	(9,100)	(11,400)	(12,800)	(9,300)	(9,200)
Closing balance	5,200	6,400	(1,500)	(2,000)	400

Table 20:1 shows that there is a mismatch in receipts and payment that creates a deficit in month 3 and 4. These need to be recovered by one

or more of the following: cash investment; the use of overdraft facility (a temporary loan). The deferral of purchases or payment and the acceleration of receipts that arrive in month 5 (perhaps by offering discounts for early settlement).

Investment Opportunities

Investment of cash involves selecting the right assets at the right time at a right place. Most capital investment decisions will have a direct effect on future profitability either because they will result in an increase in efficiency and a reduction in cost. Whatever level of management authorizes a capital expenditure the proposed investment should be properly evaluated and found to worthwhile, before the decision is taken to go ahead with the expenditure.

Capital expenditure differ from day to day revenue expenditure for the following reasons: they often involve a bigger outlay of money; the benefits will accrue over a long period of time, usually over a period over one year and often much longer. This means that the benefits can not all be set against costs in the current year's profit and loss account.

The Accounting Rate of Return (ARR)

The accounting rate of return method of appraising a capital project is to estimate the ARR or return on investment (ROI) that the project should yield that exceeds a target rate of return then that project can be undertaken.

$$ARR = \frac{(\text{Estimated Average Profits x 100})}{(\text{Estimated Average Investments})}$$

Payback Period

When deciding between two or more competing projects the usual decision is to accept the one with shortest payback period. Pay back is commonly used as the screening method to ascertain how long will it take to pay back its cost? The organization might have a target pay back and so it would reject a capital project unless its payback period is less than a certain number of years depending on the company policy.

However, a project should not be evaluated on the basis of payback alone. They pay back should not be evaluated on the screening process and if a project passes the pay back test it aught then to be evaluated using another investment appraisal technique. The reason why pay back should not be used on its own to evaluate capital investment should be clear if you look at the figures below for two mutually exclusive projects.

Discounted Cash Flow

As noted above the ARR method of project evaluation ignores the timing of cash flows and the opportunity cost of capital tied up. Payback considers the time it takes to recover the original investment cost, but ignores total profits over a project's life. The DCF is an investment appraisal technique which takes into account both timing value of money and also total profitability over project's life. So DCF is superior to both ARR and payback as the timing of cash flows is taken account by discounting them.

Internal rate of Return

The IRR is to calculate the exact rate of return which the project is expected to achieve that is the discount rate at which the NPV is 0. If the expected rate of return exceeds the target rate of return the project should be undertaken.

$$\frac{a \;+\; x}{x \;-\; y} \;\; x \;\; (b\text{-}a)$$

- A is a lower rate of return and b is the higher rate return
- X is the + NPV
- Y is the – NPV

The following cash flows have been estimated for a project:

Year	Cash flow ('000)
0	(MK2000)
1	400
2	600
3	700
4	600
5	500

It is require calculating the project NPV and stating whether the project is acceptable assuming that the cost of capital is either: 10% or 20%

a) **NPV when the cost of capital is 10%**
2000 + (400x0.909) + (600x0.826) + (700x0.751) + (600x.683) + (500x.621) = MK105.

b) **NPV when cost of capital is 20%**
2000 + (400x.833) + (600.694) + (700x0.579) + (600c.482) + (500x.402) = -MK355

$$\frac{a + x}{x - y} \quad x \quad (b\text{-}a)$$

$$= \frac{10\%+105}{105--355} \quad x \quad (20\text{-}10)$$

$$= \quad 12.3\%$$

Stock Market Ratios

If a company is listed on the stock market the investors will be interested in the market price of securities, return that a security has obtained in the past, expected future return and security.

HOW DO YOU MEASURE

1. *The dividend Yield*

This measure the expectation of expected return on the dividend invested in the stock market.

For example: given a dividend of 20 as nominal value and the market price of

$$\frac{\$\,20}{\$300} = 6.6\%$$

2. *Earnings per share*

It is a profit in tambala attributed to each equity share. Profit available to distribution. Profit after divide by total number of ordinary shares.

Example:

Profit a before tax	MK 9,320,000
Tax	MK 2,800,000
Ordinary shares (10000000, K1)	MK 10,000,000
8% Preference shares	2, 0000,000
Total capital	12,000,000

Calculate EPS

Profit before tax	9,320,000
Tax	(2,800,000)
Profit after tax	6,520,000
8% (8%x2000000)	6,360,000

$$\frac{6,360,000}{10,0000}$$
= 63.6t/ share

3. *Price earnings ratio*

P/E ratio is the most reflects the market yardstick for assessing the worth of a share

Calculated as:

$$\frac{\text{market price}}{\text{EPS}}$$

Value of price / earnings reflects the market appraisal of the shares future prospects.

If one company has a higher P/E ratio than it is because the investors either expect its earning faster than the others or considered that it is a less risky company. If the company has 30t per share and the market price is MK3.60

$$P/E = \frac{360}{30t} = 12$$

This means that the price is 12 times EPS and would take 12 years to realize the returns. The changes in P/E ratio overtime will depend on several factors including the following: if interests will go up investors will be attracted away from shares and into debt capital. If prospects for company profit improve shares prices will go up and P/E ratio will rise. Investors' confidence might be changed by the variety of circumstances such as prospect of change in Government.

4. *Dividend Cover*

This is the number of times the actual dividend could be paid out of current profits (earning). A high dividend cover means that high proportion of profits are being retuned which might indicate that the company is investing to achieve earnings growth in future.

$$\frac{\text{EPS}}{\text{D/Share}}$$

Assuming earnings are 75t/share and dividend per share is 15t/share

$$= \frac{75t}{15t}$$
$$= 5 \text{ times}$$

CHAPTER 21

Production and Operations Management

We are what we repeatedly do excellence the is not an act but a habit

What is production and operations managements?

PRODUCTION AND OPERATIONS MANAGEMENT involves planning, coordinating, and executing of all activities that create goods or provide services. The subject matter is fascinating and timely; productivity, quality, foreign competition, and customer service are very much in the news. All are part of production and operations management. Production is the process of converting, or transforming resources into goods or services.

Resources include materials, machines, money, etc. the output of production process may be manufactured goods and other services. Therefore roduction & operation management may be defined systems that create the firm's primary product of services.

Like marketing and finance, production and operations management. Is functional field of business with clear line management responsibilities? The term operations describe the set of all activities associated with the production of goods and services. Operations may involve manufacturing, in which goods are physically created from material inputs, transportation, in which the location of something or someone is changed; supply, in which the ownership or possession of goods is changed; or service, in which the principal characteristics is the treatment or accommodation to something or someone.

Why production and operations management?

You may be wondering why you need to know the importance of the production and operations management. Actually, there are these very good reasons: one is that Operations management activities are at the core of all business organizations regardless of what business they are in. it is therefore one of the major functions of any organization and is essential to understand what organization does.

We understand how people organize themselves for productive enterprise. Because we want to know how goods and services are produced. The production function is the segment of our society that creates products we use mostly costly parts of any organization. Production and Operations Management help us understand what production and operations managers do.

By understanding what these managers do can build the decision-making skills necessary to be such a manager. For example 35% or more of all jobs are in operation management related areas such areas as customer services, quality assurance, production planning and control, scheduling job design, inventory management and many more.

Activities in all of the other areas of business organization such as finance, accounting, human resources, logistics marketing, purchasing as well as others are all interrelated with operations management activities, so it is essential for these people to have a basic understanding of operations management. But beyond all of this is the reality that production/operations management is about management and all managers need to possess the knowledge and skills in the content areas you will learn about here. Among them are productivity, strategy, forecasting, quality, inventory control, scheduling, etc. also you will learn how to use decision making. Many believe that reversing the trend in manufacturing competitiveness requires more effective management of operations.

Operations management is now "where the action is". Only a few people have chosen careers in that area. There is now a shortage of skilled managers who understand the critical issues in P/OM. The service sector represents the most rapidly growing segment of the workforce. Issues of productivity and quality in providing services have become increasingly important.

Operations Strategy

Many companies neglected to include operation strategy in their corporation strategy. Some of the paid dearly for that neglected. Now more and more companies are recognizing the importance of operations strategy on the overall success of their business strategy.

Total Quality Management (TQM) – many firms are now adopting a total quality management approach to their business under this approach, the entire organization from the chief executive down becomes committed to, and involved in, a never-ending quest to improve the quality of goods and services. Key features often include a team approach, finding and eliminating problems, emphasis on serving the customer, and continuously working to improve the system.

Flexibility – The ability to adapt quickly to changes in volume of demand, I the mix of products demanded, and in product design, has become a major competitive strategy in manufacturing, the term agile manufacturing is sometimes used to connote flexibility.

Time reduction – many companies are focusing efforts on reducing the time needed to accomplish various tasks in order to gain a competitive edge.

If two companies can provide the same product at the same time price and quality, but one can deliver it four weeks earlier than the other, the quicker company will invariably get the sale.

Time reductions are being achieved in processing, information retrieval, product design, and the response to customer complaints.

Technology – technological advances have led to a vast array of new products and processes.

The computer has had, and will continue to have the greatest impact on business organisations. It has truly revolutionized the way companies operate. Applications include product processing and communication. Technological advances in new materials, new methods, and ne equipment have reducing productivity.

Worker involvement – more and more companies are pushing the responsibility for decision making and problem solving to lower levels in the organization. The reason for this trend include recognition of the knowledge workers possess about the production process and the contribution they can make to improve the production system. A key to worker involvement is the use of teams of works who solve problems and make decisions on a consensus basis.

Reengineering – some companies are taking drastic measures to improve their performance. They are conceptually starting from scratch in redesigning their processes. Business reengineering means starting over, asking why a company does things the way it is does, and questioning basic rules and assumption. Engineering focuses on significantly improving business process, such as the steps required to fill a customer's request or steps required to bring a new product to market.

Corporate downsizing – squeezing by competition, lagging productivity and stockholders calling for improved profits and share prices, many corporations have operations by reducing their labor to find ways to produce more with fewer workers. Supply chain management – Organizations are increasing their attention to managing the supply chain, from supplies and buyers of raw materials all the way to final customers. Lean production – incorporates a number of the recent trends listed here, with an emphasis on quality, flexibility, time reduction, and teamwork. This has led to a flattering of the organizational structure with fewer levels of management.

CHAPTER 22

Strategic Marketing Management

*There is no one that has
succeeded without thinking*

MARKETING is both a philosophy of business and an important function in the operation of a company. Marking is concerned with making profits by providing customer satisfaction. Thus when people buy products or services they do not using the product or service, product and services help to solve customers' problem. It is the solutions to these problems that customers are rally buying.

What is marketing?

Marketing is defined as the process of planning and executing conception, pricing, promotion and distribution of ideas, goods and services to create exchanges that satisfy individual and organization goals. Marketing is the performance of activities that seek to accomplish an organization's objectives b anticipating customer or client needs and directing a flow of need satisfying goods and services from producer to customer or client. Marketing is the management process responsible for identifying, anticipating and satisfying customers' requirement profitably. therefore marketing is more than selling and advertising

Once you have basic right one now embark on sales and marking. No business can succeed without making sales. Generate new clients while keeping retaining and grow existing ones. Remember the bird in your hand is better than the ones flying in the air. Business is about repeat business.

Treat your customers/clients with respect as if your business cannot do without them. While you chase the new customers do not forget the existing ones. There must be people that go out to sell. This is a call to create a brand, business name, identity, logo, fliers, brochures that have information about your product.

Design letter head, business cards and do market research on product, market, customer and networking/socialize as an excellent way of getting customer. Come up with a name that separates you from the rests. Build business with long term relationship. Without relationship there is no business especially repeat business. Remember that customer services are what keep the client in your books. A customer is the reason for our existence. Without that customer you will be out of business.

Development of present day marketing

In early industrial and commercial developments the emphasis was placed on production. Demand was high and all that was manufactured could be sold without difficulty. Later the emphasis switched to sales. With reduction in consumer demand, effort had to be made to sell factory output. Roughly the period from the 1920s to 1950s, was characterized by this sales orientation. Thus sales and advertising were the activities receiving most emphasis. Later the 1950s to the present day with ever increasing competitor activity and consumer needs and wants should initiate the production process.

Thus a marketing orientation developed and this is the current situation. However, it is important to recognize that not all organization adapted the marketing orientation and in most cases corporate failure can be directly attributed to companies having a production orientation approach. On one hand businesses that have production orientation have the following characteristics: demand is a function of supply: there is an emphasis on production, the firm has inward looking approach, most things made can be sold, buyers are sensitive to price, market must have low cost, with sales orientation, selling the output of production become the most import ant activity.

On the other hand business that follow market orientation have the following characteristics: they have scarcity of markets, have a focus on customers, have an outward looking approach, have high level of competitors activity and their supply exceeds demand.

Organizations adopting a marketing orientation or the marketing concept are therefore interested in the satisfaction of consumer needs and wants at a profit.

Market concept

Marketing concept is concerned with satisfying consumer needs and wants at a profit. Therefore business is about satisfying customers at a profit. So any company implementing the marketing concept will achieve their corporate objectives by identifying and satisfying the needs and want of a target markets more effectively than competitors. Effective marketing starts with the recognition of customer needs and then works backwards to devise products or services to satisfy these needs.

In this way marketing managers can satisfy customers more efficiently in the anticipate changes in customer needs more accurately in the future. This means that organization should focus on building long term customer relations in which initial sale is viewed as a beginning step in the process, not as an end goal.

Marketing mix

Marketing involves making a number of interrelated decisions about various aspects of company activity, which have a major impact on success or failure of the company as a business enterprise. The term marketing mix is used to denote the range of activities within framework of marketing decision making. The marketing mix is the set of controllable variables that must be managed to satisfy the target market and achieve organization objectives.

For convenience, the market mix is divided into four major decision areas: Product, Price, promotion and place decision.

1. Product Decision

These include the number, type, brand grouping and quality of company products, their sizes, variety and form of parking. Decision on whether to add new products, phase out products, restyle or rebrand fall into this category.

2. Price decision

These include the discount structure, the relationship of price between product sizes, the general pricing policy and the pricing of new product.

3. Promotion decision

These include advertising strategy, media selection, copy writing, public relations, personal selling sales promotions, all involving the conveyance of information about the company

4. Place decision

These include decision relation to the distribution channels and the appointment of agents among other things. The effective use of the marketing tools within the marketing mix is an interrelated manner and is the key to successful marketing and profitable business. The aim of marketing management is to get the right product of the right quality to right place at the right price using the right promotional methods. Marketing management is therefore the process of putting into practice the marketing mix- known as the 4ps.

To manage this process it involves analysis, planning and control. As we have seen marketing orientation begins and ends with the customer. Thus analysis in marketing management involves finding the answer to the following questions: Who are our customer and potential customers? Who do they buy (or not buy). Do they buy our product or services? When do they buy it? Where do they buy it? How customers are needs changing? Which of the competitor's product do they consider buying? Marketing management also involves using the information gained from market analysis to plan the organization's marketing response/activities. The third main component of the marketing management is to control the operationalization of marketing plan. Control involves setting measurable tar targets. If necessary remedial action will need to be taken to ensure that planning and actual performance are brought into line.

Internal Marketing

As part of the overall marketing process of delivering customer satisfaction and committed to achieving this objective. In practice this means that all employees at all levels should appreciate not only the reason for the firm's existence: but also that each and every employee has a responsibility to understand the concept of customer or marketing orientation and the importance of their individual contribution.

How marketing relates to production

Although production is necessary economic activity, some people overrate its importance in relation to marketing. Production and marketing are both importance parts of a total business system aimed at providing consumers with need-satisfying goods and services. Simply put take out marketing there will no production. Together, production and marketing supply five kinds of economic utility.

1. Form utility: Form utility is provide when someone produces something tangible (things you can touch or see)
2. Task utility: Task utility is provided when someone performs a task for someone else. thus marketing decisions focus on services customer and include decision about what goods and services to produce. It doesn't make sense to provide goods and services consumers don't want when they are so many things they do want. Marketing is concerned with what customers' want- and should guide what is production combine to provide form or task utility, consumer won't be satisfied utility possession, time and place utility are also provided.
3. Possession utility: Possession utility means obtaining a good or service and having the right to use or consumer it.
4. Time utility : Time utility means having the product available when the customer wants
5. Place utility: Place utility means having the product available

Market strategy planning

Market strategy planning means finding attractive opportunities and developing profitable marketing strategies. Marketing strategy what is it? A market strategy specifies a target market and a relate marketing mix. A target market is a fairly homogeneous (similar) group of customer to who accompany wishes to appeal

Marketing plan

The marketing plan is a guide to implementation and control. Marketing plan fills out marketing strategy. A market strategy sets a target market and a marketing mix. So a marketing plan is a written statement strategy and the time related details for carrying out the strategy.

Thus the marketing plan should spell out: what marketing mix will be offered; to whom (the target market) and for how long. What company resource will be need at what rate and the plan should also include some control procedures.

After the marketing plan is developed, a marketing manager knows what needs to be done the marketing manager is concerned with implementation – putting marketing plans into operation. Control is simply analyzing and correction what you have done. Therefore at the heart of the market plan we find situation analysis, marketing objectives, target market selection, market mix (The 4Psof marketing) and implementation and control.

Marketing activities must be aligned with organizational objectives and marketing opportunities are often found by systematically analyzing situation environments. Once an opportunity is recognized, the marketing manager must then plan an appropriate strategy for taking advantage of the opportunity. This process can be viewed in terms of: establishing marketing objectives, selecting the target market and developing the marketing mix.

What are the attractive opportunities?

There are breakthrough opportunities. These help innovators to develop hard to copy marketing strategies that will be very profitable for a long time and enhance competitive, product development, diversification strategies. International opportunities should be considered (Getting an advantage of internationalization).For the market to be attractive should show competiveness, should be robust and consistent.

Establishing the market objectives

Marketing objectives are usually derived from organizational objectives. Marketing objectives are stated as standards of performance (e.g. A certain percentage of market share or sales volume). While such objectives are useful, the marketing concept emphasizes the profits rather than sales should be overriding objectives providing the framework for marketing plan.

The marketing objectives

Market objectives include: increase the market share, continuity of profits, enlarging the market, harvesting and establishing market position.

Selecting Target Market

The success of any marketing plan hinges on how well it can identify customer needs and organizes its resources to satisfy them profitably. Four important questions must be answered: What do customers want and need? What must be done to satisfy these wants? What is the size of the market? What is the growth profile?

Getting Information for Marketing Decision

Marketing managers need information for implementation and control. Without good information managers will be forced to guess which is detrimental in today's fast changing markets. Information goes at a price and in some cases providers of the information (customers and competitors) can be unpredictable. The manager should therefore decide what information is critical and how to get it. Marketing information systems (M.I.S) is an organized way of continually gathering and analyzing data to provide marketing managers with the information they need to make decisions.

Relationship Marketing

A marketing orientation focuses on the needs of a customer first of all. Relationship marketing emphasizes views that companies survive and prosper by selling more goods to the same customer. Customers that purchase regularly develop expectations of the supplier. A customer must be turned from a one off purchaser to an advocate. The underlying principle of relationship marketing is that repeat business is more profitable. It costs less to sell to existing customers.

Market research

The concept of marketing says that marketing managers should meet the needs of customers. Research provides a bridge to customers and this means marketing managers have to rely on help from marketing research. Marketing research involves procedures to develop and analyze new information which will help marketing managers to make decision. Effective researches requires cooperation between marketing managers and researchers and of ethical issues exist in marketing research and have to be considered by marketing managers in their decision.

Market research and the Scientific method

Scientific method is a decision making approach that focuses on being objective and orderly in testing ideas before accept them. Managers do not assume that their intuition is correct. They rather use their intuition and observation to develop a hypothesis. In simple terms a hypothesis is an educated guess about the relationship between things or about what will happen in the future. The hypothesis is then tested before making final decision. Scientific method helps marketing managers to make better decision.

Marketing research includes the following five steps: defining the problem; analyzing the situation; getting problem specific data; interpreting the data and solving the problem.

CHAPTER 23

People management

THE PRACTICE OF PEOPLE MANAGEMENT is concerned with all aspects of how people are employed and managed in organizations. It covers activities such as strategic Human Resource Management; human capital management; corporate social responsibility; knowledge management, organizational management; resourcing (human resource planning, recruitment and selection and talent management); performance management; learning and development reward management; Employee relations; Health and safety and Provision of employee services

For the purpose soft this chapter we will use the term Human Resource Management interchangeably with the term people management.

Human Resource Management Defined

A plethora of human resource management definitions has emerged. Stone defines Human Resource Management as a productive use of people to achieve strategic business objectives and satisfy individual employee needs. According to Armstrong (2009) Human Resource Management is a strategic, integrated and coherent approach to the employment, development and wellbeing of people working in an organization

However, other scholars say that human resource involves all management decisions and action that affect the nature of the relationship between the organization and its employees-its human resources. Boxall et al (2007)

HRM as the management of work and people towards desired ends. Storey (1988) concurs with Boxall at al (2007) by believing that HRM can be regarded as interrelated policies within ideological and philosophical underpinning.

This means that HRM comprises a set of policies designed to maximize organizational integration, employee commitment, flexibility and quality of work. Therefore, it can be concluded that HRM consist of the following propositions:

1. That Human Resource policies should be integrated with strategic business planning
2. That human resource is a distinct approach to employment management which seeks to achieve competitive advantage through the strategic deployment of a highly committee and capable workforce.
3. That HRM is concerned with how organizations manage their workforce.

Aims of HRM

The overall purpose of human resource management is to ensure that the organization is able to achieve success through people. As Ulrich and Lake Remark HRM systems can be source of organizational capabilities that allow firms to learn and capitalize on new opportunities'

Personnel Vs HRM

HRM is long term or proactive. HRM is strategic while a personnel Management is Adhoc. HRM is Unitarist (focuses on an individual) while personnel Management is bureaucratic. HRM is largely integrated into line management while Personnel Management is specialist.

HR Strategy

The concept of strategic is based on a number of associated concepts; Competitive advantage, resource-based strategy, distinctive capabilities, strategic intent, Strategic capability, Strategic management, Strategic goals and strategic plans.

Competitive Advantage

The concept of competitive advantage was formulated by Michael porter (1985). Competitive advantage porter asserts arise out of a firm creating value for its customers. To achieve it, firms choose markets in which they can excel and present a moving target to their competitors by continually improving their position. Poter emphasized on the importance of generic strategies (low cost leadership, differentiation and focus) the organization can use to gain h competitive advantage.

Distinctive Capabilities

As a kay comments, the opportunity for companies to sustain a competitive advantage is determined by their capabilities. A distinctive capability or competence can be described as an important feature that confers superiority of the organization. Kay extends this definition by emphasizing that there is a difference between distinctive capabilities and producible capabilities.

On one hand distinctive capabilities are those characteristics that cannot be replicated by competitors or can only be initiated with great difficulty. On the other hand, reproducible capabilities are those that can be bought or created by any company with reasonable management skills, diligence and financial resources.

Prahand and Hamel argue that competitive advantage stems in the long term when a firm builds core competences that are superior to those of its rivals and when it learns faster and applies its learning more effectively than its competitors. Distinctive capabilities or core competences describe what the organization is specially or uniquely of doing.

Strategic intent

In its simplest form strategy may be described as an expression of intentions of the organization-what it means to do and how to do. This means that business means to get from here to there. Strategic refers to the expression of the leadership position the organization wants to attain and establishes a clear criterion on how progress towards its achievement will be measured.

Strategic Capabilities

A strategic capability is the concept that refers to the ability of the organization to develop and implement strategies that will achieve sustained competitive advantage. It is therefore about the capacity to define realistic intentions, to match resources to opportunities and to prepare and implement strategic plans. People who display high levels of strategic capability know where they are going and how they are going to get there.

Resource Based View

The resource-based view of strategy is that the strategic capability of a firm depends on its resource capability. Boxall comments, competitive success does not come simply by making choices in the present. It stems from building up distinctive capabilities over significant periods of time.

What are HR Strategies?

HR strategies set out what the organization intents to do about its human resource management policies and practices about its human resource management policies and practices and how they should be integrated with the business strategy. They are defined by dyer and Reserves as 'internally consistent bundles of human resource practices, The purpose of HR strategies is to articulate what an organization intends to do about its human resources management policies and practices now and in longer term. This means that business and managers should perform well in the present to succeed in the future. Thus HR strategies aim to meet both business and human resource need in the business organization.

However, because all organizations are different, all HR strategies are different. There is no such a thing as a standard strategy and research into HR strategy conducted by Armstrong and Long revealed many variations. Some strategies are imply very general declarations of intent.

Purpose of HR Strategy

To articulate what van organization intends to do about its human resource now and in the long term. General HR Strategy Areas include: High Performance Management; High Committed Management; Corporate Social Responsibility; Organization Development Engagement; Knowledge Management; Learning and Development; Reward; Employee Relations and Employee-Wellbeing

How HR Strategies Can Be Implemented

To implement HR strategies there is need to analyze business needs and how the HR Strategy will help to meet them. Then communicate full information on the strategy and what it expected to achieve. You also need to involve those concerned in identifying implementation problems and how they should be dealt with in line with action plans. Finally, plan and execute a program of project management that ensures that action plans are achieved.

CHAPTER 24

Diligence in Business

GOD'S ORDAINED ASSIGBNMENT is not for the idle. Diligence simply means hard work. This means that whatever God has called you to do, pursue it diligently. In other words you need to go about your vision with all diligence. Progress in life is a function of hard work. There is no food for a lazy man anywhere in this world.

> **Seest thou a man diligent in his business; he shall stand before kings; he shall not stand before mean men**
> Proverbs 22:29

Lazy and idle people never make headway in life, because they are not operating God's formula for successful living. Such people failure, disappointment and frustration is their portion. Victory and success will not find you in the house you have to go out and search for it.

> **Blessed shalt thou be when thou come in and blessed shalt thou be when thou goes out**
> Deuteronomy 28:6

This is a call not to sit down in your home and watch video the whole day. You will fail to bring food on the table. Even if you pray, fast and speak in tongues food will not come. Isaac in the book of Genesis was a hard worker in the land of philistines. He did not say that because it is God who sent me here then I don't have to work. The bible says sowed in the land and in the same year he reaped a hundred-fold.

> **...Received in the same year a hundred-fold: and the lord blessed him ... And the man waxed great, and went forward, and grew until he became very great**
> Gen 26:12-13

It is God who prospers these that work hard. From the aforementioned scripture God prospered Isaac to HE will prosper you too in your head work and not in your laziness.

And if a man also strives for masteries yet is he not crowned except he strive lawfully.

2 Timothy 2:15.

Laziness is a destroyer and it puts man to a state of lack of and begging. The more you engage yourself in diligence the better you become. It is more difficult to locate to the top without being diligent. I know many that are run the race but it is only one that receives the price.

"He becometh poor that dealeth with a slack hand: but the hand of the diligent maketh rich"

Proverbs 10:4

Everyone that receives the price in a competition does so after hard work. So, you need press on and be diligent. It goes without saying that if you will not run and you do not work either from your own business or employment you will not eat. The basis of an increase is output. If you are not a worker today be assured that tomorrow you will be a beggar and borrower that fail to pay back

"The wicked borrows and does not pay back but the righteous gracious and gives"

Psalms 37:21

If this happens to you and then you are dragged into a situation where you fail to bring food on the table, going without eating and reduced to a beggar what a shame.

For even we were with you, this we commanded you, that if any would not work, neither should he eat

Thessalonians 3:10

God says the labor is worthy of his hirer

(Luke 10:7)

He is worth of his wages. So, what do you do to receive wages? Just labor. From this day do not go to bed with un accomplished list of items on your daily list. Life does not give you what you deserve thus why you must fight for it.

CHAPTER 25

Ethics in Business

You must be the change you wish to see in the world

MANY BUSINESS COMMENTATORS say that business ethics is critical and is a structure examination of how people and institutions should behave in the world of commerce. In particular, involves examining appropriate constraints on the pursuit of self-interest, or (for firms) profits, when the actuations of individuals or firms affect others. At the heart of business ethics is rightness and wrongness. For example, is it right to engage in insider trading? Is it morally right to be involved in corporate lies? However, many businesses commentators say that business ethics is the discipline of applying general ethical dilemmas in business dealings. According to Chris (2009) "BUSINESS ETHICS" is the study of ethical dilemmas, values and decision-making in the world of commerce. It applies to all aspects of business conduct and is relevant to the conduct of individuals and business organizations as a whole.

Business ethics (also called as corporate ethics) is a form of professional ethics that examines ethical principles and moral or ethical problems that arise in a business environment. Applied ethics is a field of ethics that deals with ethical questions in many fields such as medical, technical, legal and business ethics

Business ethics can be both normative and a descriptive discipline. As a corporate practice and career specialization, the field is primarily normative. The range and quantity of business ethical issues reflects the degree to which business is perceived to be at odds with non-economic social values.

Business Ethics and the Changing Environment

Businesses and governments operate in changing technological, legal, economical social and political environments. With competing stakeholders and power claims. Stakeholders are individuals, companies, groups and nations that cause and respond to: external issues, opportunities and threats.

Internet and information technologies globalization, deregulation, mergers and wars, have acceralated rate of change and uncertainty. In today's dynamic and complex environment stakeholders such as professionals, shareholders management employees, consumer's suppliers and members of community must make and manage business and moral decisions.

Environment Forces and Stakeholders

Organizations are embedded in and interact with multiple changing local, national and international environments. These environments are increasingly moving toward and emerging into global system of dynamic interrelated interactions among local, national and international. A first step toward understanding stakeholder issues is to gain an understanding of environmental forces that influence issues and stakes of different groups. This is a call to think globally before acting locally in many situations. As we discuss an overview of these environmental forces here, think of the effects and pressures each of the forces has on your industry, company, profession or career and job.

Stakeholder Management Approach

The question is: how do companies, communication media, political groups, consumers, employees, competitors, and other groups respond when they are affected by an issue, dilemma, threat or opportunity from one or more of the environments described? The stakeholder management approach is a way of understanding the effects of environmental forces and groups on specific issues that affect real-time stakeholders and their welfare.

The stakeholder approach begins to address these questions by enabling individuals and groups to articulate collaborative win-win strategies. The underlying aims here is to develop awareness of the ethics and responsibility of different stakeholders' perceptions, plans strategies and actions.

Business ethics: Why does it Matter?

Business ethicists ask. "What is right and wrong, good and bad, and harmful and beneficial regarding decisions and actions in and around organizational activities? Ethical "solutions" to business and organizational problems may seem available. Thus to first be aware and recognize a potential problem.

"Doing the right thing" matters to all stakeholders. To companies and employees, acting legally and ethically means saving billions of dollars each year in lawsuits settlements and significant financial penalties for acting unethically. Costs to business also include: deterioration of relationships; damage to reputation; declining employee productivity; loyalty and absenteeism; companies that have a reputation of unethical and uncaring behavior toward employees also have a difficult time recruiting and retaining valued professionals.

For business leaders and managers, managing ethically also means managing with integrity. Integrity cascades throughout an organization an. It shapes and influences the values, tone and culture of the organization, commitment and imagination of everyone in the company. Then we can evaluate our own and other's values, assumptions and judgments regarding the problem before we act. Laura Nash points that business ethics deals with three basic areas of managerial decisions making. First, is a choice about what the laws should be and whether to follow them. Second, choices about economic and social issues outside the domain of law, and lastly choices about the priority of self-interest over the company's interest.

What are Unethical Business Practices?

Surveys identify prominent everyday ethical issues facing businesses and their stakeholders. Recurring themes include: managers lying to employees or vice versa; office favoritism; taking credit for others' work; receiving or offering kickbacks; stealing from the company, firing an employee for whistle blowing. Padding expenses accounts to obtain reimbursements for questionable business expenses; divulging confidential information or trade secrets commonly called insider trading; terminating employment without giving sufficient notice and using company property and materials for personal use.

9 Things That Ethics Promotes

- Openness and transparency
- Honesty and integrity
- Excellence and quality
- Public accountability
- Legality
- Promote justice
- Confidential information
- Balanced decisions
- Whistle blowing

Relativism

Although relativism is most often associated with ethics, one can find defenses of relativism in virtually any area of philosophy. Both relativism and morality involve the field of ethics, also called moral philosophy, which involves systematic, defending and recommending concepts of right and wrong behavior.

The term ethics is also us defined as a discipline involving inquiry into more judgments people make and ten rules and principles upon which such judgments are based. There are two different versions of relativism: Factual Moral Relativism (FRM) and Normative Ethical Relativism (NER) as it is often claimed that moral beliefs are in fact relative.

It will be useful to generalize a distinction familiar from discussions of ethical relativism and to distinguish FMR and NER with respect to anything that is claimed to be relative. Moral beliefs are in fact relative, that the different people do make different moral judgments and advocates different moral rules and principles. Thus, FMR claims about moral ideas and the like are often counted by arguments that such things are universal. Therefore, FMR are empirical claims may tempt us to conclude that they are little philosophical interests, but there are several reasons why thus is so. This position is called FMR and as factual matter, the truth of FMR can be decided by empirical investigation. On the other hand, Normative Ethical Relativism (NER) is acclaim that an Act in society S is right if and only if most people in society S believe A is right.

This is a Universal Normative Principal in so far as it implies to any person in society. However, the possibility of NER arises only when some action or practices is the locus of disagreement between holders of two self-contained and exclusive systems. For example, the two system beliefs S1 and S2 are exclusive of one another when they have consequences that disagree under some description but do not require either to abandon their side of the disagreement. Thus, a real confrontation between S1and S2 would occur in real option for the group living under S.

From the forgoing discussion we can conclude that NER seems to be a less powerful tool not robust enough and less convincing since in both society S1 and fails to understand why the same tool is interpreted differently. However, it is argued that if the principal of tolerance is accepted the society groups need to neither impose nor foster tolerance is accepted the society groups need not impose nor foster tolerance on moral beliefs on others.

On such NER can be accepted because it is the only normative principal with commitment to tolerance. To their concepts, beliefs or modes of reasoning, then groups can not differ with respect to their concepts, beliefs or modes of reasoning. Further, the NER supported by FMR takes on a more practical task, which is to arrive on one hand FMR does not necessarily deny the existence of a single correct moral appraisal, given the same set of circumstances. This means that FMR as a tool for supporting NER with empirical investigation NER in a given area tends to counsel tolerance of practices that conform to alternatives standards prevailing in the area.

On the other hand, FMR input into NER claims that different cultures have different views of morality, which they unify under one general conception of morality. FMR presupposes some measure of realism. For example, if there are no such things as concepts, beliefs or modes of reasoning, then groups cannot differ with respect at more standards that regulate right and wrong conduct. Thus, this may involve articulating the good habit that we should acquire, the duties that we should following consequences of our behavior on others.

Ethical Theory

COGNITIVISM AND NON-COGNITIVISM

The first and most profound division in ethical theory is between the claim that it is possible to know moral right from wrong and denial of that claim. Because this is claim and counter-claim about what we can and cannot know, the position which declares we can know is called 'cognitivism' and the contrary position 'non cognitivism'. According to cognitivism there are objective moral truths which can be known, just as we can know other truths about this world. Statements of moral belief, on this view can be true or false just as our statement that something is certain color can be true or false. According to the non-cognivist, by contrast, 'objective' assessment of moral belief is not possible.

It is all 'subjective'. There is no truth or falsity to be discovered. There's only belief, attitude, emotional reaction, and the like. As Hamlet puts it, there is nothing either good or bad but thinking makes it so'. When non-cognitivism claims that there are only attitudes, its proponents do not usually mean that moral judgments are simply expressions one's feelings. Advocates of non-cognitivism acknowledge the essentially social nature of morality by invariably arguing that these are group attitudes.

Consequentialism Versus Non-Consequentialism

The greatest divide in cognivist thinking is between theories which assess moral right and wrong in terms of the consequences of actions and those which do not. Those which do are 'consequentialist' theories; those which do not are 'non consequentialist. With consequentialist theories we look to the results of actions to determine the truth or falsity of moral judgments about them. If what follows from an action is, on balance of benefit then it is, a good action and so we are right to do it. Conversely, if the outcome is, on balance harmful then the action is 'bad' and we are 'wrong' do it.

For consequentialism the test of whether an action is right or wrong is whether it is good or bad in the sense of resulting in benefit or harm. In this case right or wrong is a question of good or bad; and good or bad a question of benefit or harm. For non-consequentialism, there is no immediate appeal to beneficial or harmful consequences to determine good or bad. A Divine Command theory offers an illustration of the difference between consequentialism and non-consequentialism.

If religious believers were to obey God's commands in order to attain a desirable state after death, or because they believed that obedience was rewarded by material success. Then such moves presuppose a consequentialist view of ethic. If, however, the believer obeys God's commands, not for any expected reward, but for the sole reason that God has commanded them, then he or she presupposes a strictly non-consequentialist account of morality. It is not what follows from our actions which then make them right or wrong but only the fact of their conformity to God's commands.

It is solely in virtue of being activities of such as a conforming kind that actions are right or wrong and therefore good or bad. Taken item by item, a consequentialist and non-consequentialist listing of rights and wrongs will probably not differ very much. Of course, there will be some disagreement on substantive moral issues and they are, unsurprisingly, likely to concern just those issues that divide society the most.

Utilitariasm:

AN ETHICAL OF WELFARE

The best-known consequentialist theory of ethics is called 'utilitarianism'. The name derives from the use of the word utility to denote the capacity in actions to have good results. This choice of word utility to denote the capacity in actions to have good results. This choice of word proclaims the consequentialist nature of the theory. Utility means usefulness-underlying the point that it is the usefulness of actions which determines their moral character than anything in the nature of the action itself.

Actions are not good or bad in themselves, but only in what they are good or bad for. Although, strictly speaking, good and dad are the results, while utility and disutility are the capabilities for those results, they amount to the same thing in practice and can, for convenience, be treated as synonymous.

PART IV

SECRETS OF SUCCESS

CHAPTER 26

Business Success Secrets

Create A Winning Recipe

After some trial and error in your business,you will figure out what works best. Once that that happens, you will want to the same thing over and over again. This is your recipe for success. Just like food recipe, a business recipe can be followed time and again to achieve the same result. In fact, some believe that that's why money is called dough; you make your dough by using a recipe. In your business, your business dough recipe could be:

1. An ad that works
2. A monthly mailer
3. A sale that brings in customers
4. A monthly seminar
5. A stall at the Saturday public market
6. A billboard
7. Great locations
8. Almost anything that works and can be duplicated.

If you may think about it, repeating a successful formula is the hallmark of any well-run business. Budweiser sponsors sporting events because it knows that it will sell more beer if it does. Sponsoring sporting events is a tried and true business recipe. It works time and time again. Microsoft too has a recipe. We might call it "tweak and put out a new edition of Windows every few years". Microsoft knows that if it does so, it will be able to predictably count on those sales. Hollywood does the same thing. Whereas no one knows for sure what movie people will like, Hollywood knows that it reduces the risk of failure if, for example, Tom Cruise or Julia Roberts stars in it. Getting a big name to star in a movie is a business recipe.

If your business going to be a long-term success, you will need to do the same thing. What will your recipe be? You need to experiment and figure out what works best. After you do, long term success will be much more likely if you reduce that thing, whatever it is, to a formula that you can repeat over and over again.

In his great book The E-Myth: Why most Small Businesses Don't work and What to Do about It, author Michael Gerber explains that many people go into business because they love something and want to make a living at it, a baker who loves to bake, for example. Gerber makes a clear that what trips up the baker is that, while what he wants is to bake, being a business owner.

Create Multiple Profit Centers

The problem for most small businesses is that they learn one good recipe, stick with it, run into the ground and never bother to figure out another one. The owner has learned only one method of making a buck. The problem with having just a single moneymaking formula is that it will inevitably be hit when the dreaded business cycle turns south.

Just like the economy, all businesses have a business cycle. The ice cream store sees sales spike in the summer and drop in the winter. Starbucks sees sales rise in the winter and drop in the summer. While experience will teach you, often the hard way, what your business cycle is, you can learn it much easier by speaking with people in your own line of work who have been around for a while. Once you know what your business cycle is, either through research or the school of hard knocks, you will want to minimize its effects on your business. One of the best ways to do that that is to create multiple profit centers, a term coined by Barbara Winter in her book, making a living without a Job.

The theory is essentially this: To succeed long term in business, you need several recipes. You need to diversify your income. A smart stock investor does just that. He knows not to buy just one stock. That stock may go up, but it may down. Having more than one stock ensures that when one stock does go down, the likelihood of taking a big financial hit is remote. His income is diversified. Your business must diversify as well if you are going to last.

Seven Secrets of The Great Entrepreneurs

While the idea of being an entrepreneur may start with a flicker, it often grows very bright. Even so, the question remains: Why are some entrepreneurs more successful than others/ usually, it is because they know some things other entrepreneurs do not. Here are the seven secrets of the great entrepreneurs.

1. Be Willing to Take a Big Risk

Entrepreneurship is, as we have discussed a risk. When you quit your job to start a new business, there is no guarantee it will succeed, let alone succeed wildly; Cookie stores were nonexistence when Debbie Field opened her first one in 1977. Today, Mrs. Fields Cookies numbers more 1,000 stores. You have to be willing to look like a fool to succeed wildly in your own business (and that is the idea), you too will need to take a risk; an intelligent, calculated gamble has the chance to hit big. Of course, it can also backfire but that's why we play the game.

2. Dream Big Dreams

In the early 1950's, a young engineer named Douglas Englebart decided that work for 51/2 million minutes for someone else (the amount of time that would elapse before he would turn 65), he would rather use his career to benefit kind, he wanted to help people solve problems; that was the need he thought he could fill. Englebart had an epiphany. At a time when computers were machines the size of a room that were primarily for number crunching and had no screens at all, and despite the fact that he knew next to nothing about them, Englebart saw a future where the computer could be an interactive tool, operated by "any kind of a lever or knob, or buttons, or switches you wanted."

The vision so engrossed Douglas Englebart that he spent the next decade chasing that dream, before eventually becoming known as the father of the computer mouse. No one will give you permission to be bold, but boldness is a requirement. As W.H. Murray wrote in The Scottish Himalayan Expedition: Until one is committed, there is hesitancy, the chance to draw back, always ineffectiveness. Concerning all acts of initiative (and creation) there is one elementary truth, the ignorance that kills countless ideas and splendid plans: that the moment definitely commits oneself, and then providence moves too.

All sorts of thing occur to help one that would never otherwise have occurred. A whole stream of events issues from the decision, raising in one's favor all manner unforeseen incidents and meetings and material assistance, which no man could have dreamed would have come his way. I have learned a deep respect for one of Goethe's couplets: "Whatever you can do, or dream you can, begin it. Boldness has genius, power and magic in it."

3. Value the customer above all else

For Richard Branson, founder of the Virgin Group, the Customer is king. For instance, he believed that many record stores suffered because the shopping experience was boring and the staff needed to enjoy their jobs more. Voila! Virgin megastore was born- a place stocked to the brim that has a great vibe where you can usually listen to the music you want before you buy it. It might help to know too that Branson started out not much different than the rest of us. His first business was a record store above a shoe shop in London, and he bartered for his rent.

As Sam Walton pit it: To succeed you need to exceed your customers' expectations." Let them know you appreciate them. Make good on all your mistakes, and don't make excuses-apologize Stand behind everything you do. The two most important words I ever wrote were on that first Wal-Mart sign, 'Satisfaction Guaranteed'. They're still up there, and they have made all the difference.

4. Take Care of Your People

This includes your employees, your investors and your stockholders. In 1913, Henry Ford said, "The wages we pay are too small in comparison with our profits. I think we should raise our minimum pay rate." Moreover, eight years later Ford introduced the first five-day work week, stating, "Every man needs more than one day for rest and recreation." And if ever there was an entrepreneur who knew how to succeed, it was Ford.

5. Persevere

As I said, entrepreneurship is a risk and, as such, entrepreneurs often fail. Many successful entrepreneurs go bankrupt before they hit it big, but they stick with it anyway. In 1975, Microsoft's revenues were $16,000 and it had three employees. In 1976, revenues were $22,000 with seven employees. In both years, the company posted losses. Many companies would have quit after two such years, but most companies would have quit after two such years, but companies are not Microsoft.

6. Believe in Yourself

Buckminster Fuller, inventor of the geodesic dome and countless other tools, was an unknown, unhappy man when he decided to kill himself in 1927. But before he went through with it, he realized his problem had always been that he listened to others instead of himself. Then and there, he decided to trust his own Intuition. Before he died, Fuller had revolutionized such disparate fields as architecture, mathematics, housing and automobiles.

7. Have a Passion

A trait common to all great entrepreneurs is that they are passionate about what they do. Legendary investor and entrepreneur Charles Schwab put it this way, "The person who does not work for the love of work but only for money is not likely to make money or to find much fun in life." Similarly, Anita Roddick, founder and managing director of Body Shop International, once said, "I want to work for a company that contributes to and is part of the community. I want something not just to invest in, I want something to believe in."

In the end, maybe writer Joseph Campbell said it best, "If you follow your bliss, doors will open for you that wouldn't have opened for anyone else." That is the job before you-to find that bliss and turn it into profit. A challenge? Yes. But what a great challenge it is. The good news is that you need not to be a world-famous entrepreneur to think and act like one, and you need not reinvent the wheel either. Take from this book the ideas that you like, discard those you don't, become a great entrepreneur in your own right, and go conquer your part of the globe. Good luck!

The Bottom-line

Creating multiple profit centers is one of the smartest things you can do to ensure the long-term viability of your business. So is giving people what they want. Help is always nearby via the SBA and its affiliates. Finally, remember that boldness has genius, power and magic in it.

CHAPTER 27

Business on Shoestring

BOOTSTRAP FINANCING

YOU MAY WANT TO START a business but do not have enough money to do so. Are you out of luck? Nope. Actually, it is safe to say that most businesses tart with less than optimum funding. According to the small Business Administration (SBA),60 percent of all new businesses begin as undercapitalized start-ups. So, you are in good company. But what it will take is hard work, pluck, and a tad of luck. Creating a shoestring business begins with finding the necessary funding (discussed in this chapter).

Ten Rules For Bootstrapping A Business

If you are going to bootstrap a business, there are some rules of the road you should know. As you go about getting the money you need to get started, it will help enormously to keep these ten tips in mind.

Rule 1: You don't need a fortune to get started.

It would be great if you had enough money, but just because you don't, it doesn't mean that you can't start a business.

Rule 2: Not all debt is bad debt.

This is an injunction to Rule 1. If you don't have enough money, then it is possible that you may have to incur debt to get going. But not all debt is bad debt. Some debt is good debt when it enables you to get ahead in life-to start a business, buy a home, Finance College, etc. Most millionaires start out deeply in debt to finance their dream. Is it ideal? Of course not. But if you can take on some debt and see a way to pay it back through your business, it's not a bad option.

Rule 3: Be frugal

As an employee, you can waste supplies, make long distance calls, use FedEx, make too many copies, and spend your management budget without a second thought. But as a business person on a budget, you will have to learn to be lean and mean.

Rule 4: Invest only in your best ideas

Remember that no business survives unless it is serving a market need. You may have any ideas, but faced with less money than ideal, you cannot afford to make mistakes. You must invest your time, money and energy in only your best, most profitable ideas.

Rule 5: Do what it takes

If you only are going to have 25 percent of the money that you need to start, then you must be willing to put in the other 75 percent in the form of time and effort. You will have to work harder and smarter than your competitors. You have to be willing to go the extra mile as a boot strapper.

Rule 6: Look big

You may be starting a business out of tour garage with no funds, but no one needs to know that. It is critical to your success that you project the image of a big, professional business. Until the business does get big and have some money, remember these two important words: Fake it!

Beware of the Credit Card Trap

While you can take out cash advances from your credit cards to start your business, be careful. The credit card trap is easy to fall into but very hard to get out of. You know the trap, don't you? It follows this pattern: You charge for things you otherwise cannot afford or take out cash you have no way of paying back; You run up balances on cards that charge you 18 percent interest (and up!); You pay only the minimum due each month, covering only the interest and service charge each month; You get stuck with a debt that never seems to go down.

Here's how to get out of the trap:

- After you have run up your cards, transfer all the balances to the card with the lowest interest rate. This can save you a lot of money every month.
- Better yet, apply for a new card with a really low introductory "teaser" rate (e.g. 4.9%) and transfer all of your balances to that card.
- Once the teaser rate is set to expire, call that company and tell them that you will cancel the card unless they extend the rate for another six months. If they don't agree to do so, cancel the card, apply for another new card with a great rate, and transfer the balance again. This balance transfer dance can save you a ton of money.
- Pay off the total balance as soon as possible and always pay more than the minimum.

Rule 7: Be Creative

No money to hire that great Web designer? You better buy a book and learn a web design program. Another option: barter. Another option: hire a student. As a boot strapper, you have to constantly be on guard for new ideas and new ways to bring in a buck.

Rule 8: You got to believe

Northwestern University conducted as a study of successful shoestring entrepreneurs and discovered that they typically never owned a business before, had no business education, and of course, didn't have enough money to start but did anyway. In short, they didn't know enough to be afraid.

Rule 9: Have a passion

Wayne Huzienga started very small and eventually created Blockbuster Video, among many other businesses. Says Huzienga, "I don't think we are unique, we're certainly not smarter than the next guy. So, the only thing I can think of that we might do a little differently that some people are we work harder and when we focus in on something, we are consumed by it. It becomes a passion."

Rule 10: Take care of your customers

You may not have as much money as the next guy. You may not have ads as big or a fleet of salesmen, but that does not mean you cannot be the best. One of the best ways to be the best is to offer personal, superior service of your customers.

OPM-Other People's Money

While it is difficult to start without enough money, it can be done. A far better solution when you don't have money to start a business is to get enough money using OPM-other people's money. Finding people who will be willing to invest in you will take determination; it usually isn't easy. Without collateral, perseverance will be essential. Why? Because lenders and investors are skeptics, and they should be. Too many startups fail, so, accordingly, investors would rather put their capital into successful businesses that want to expand or start ups that have already been partially funded. The unfunded start-up is the riskiest investment of all.

But it is also, potentially, the most lucrative, and you can use that fact to your advantage. If you are willing to share your pie, have a plan that makes economic sense, and are willing to look long and hard, the right investor can be found. It is the possibility of a big return on their investment, coupled with the ability to write off a loss on their taxes, that makes the rich investor a viable alternative for the cash-strapped entrepreneur. The key will be your ability to entice the right person with the right deal. Investors want a high return. Ask them what they want, and give them what they want. Most investors will want to know what you are putting into the venture, aside from your sweat equity. Be honest. If you are donating equipment or material, say so. If you are tapping credit cards, fess up. Your commitment can only help your cause.

The key to winning over an investor or other lender is to look like a pro. Talking a big without back-up facts will make you look a fool. Instead, come in looking like a businessman who understands business. You need facts, data, and hard figures that back up your rosy rhetoric.

You must know:

- How much you really need
- Why you need that much
- How much you can afford to pay back every month
- How you will make that amount

If you can answer these questions confidently, then it is time to go over your options because there are many ways to finance your business using OPM.

Providing Great Customer Service

- Ask your customers what they want and then give it to them. Survey your clients and customers. Find out what you are doing right and wrong. Change what needs to be changed.
- Train your employees. Your employees will not know what is expected of them until you teach them.
- Empower your employees. Give employees the room to solve problems on their own. For instance, at Outback Steakhouse the wait staff can offer patrons free drinks, appetizers, or meals when something goes wrong, without asking a manager.
- Reward your employees. Employees who make customers happy are making you money. If they are rewarded for a job well done, that behavior will be reinforced.
- Do more than expected. Going above and beyond the call of duty endears you to clients. Do so consistently and your business will take off.

Structuring the Deal

When structuring a loan or investment deal, keep these points in mind:

- How much money do you need? Ask for more than you need. Either you will be able to negotiate down to the right amount or you will have more than enough to get started. Either you will be able to negotiate down to the right amount or you will have more than enough to get started. Either way, you win.
- Who is taking out the loan? Make sure that it is your company and not you personally. While you may have to give a personal guarantee for the loan, avoid doing so if at all possible.
- How much interest will you have to pay? Remember everything is negotiable.
- How long is the term? You need to run some numbers that tell you how much you can afford to repay back the loan. The longer the term, the better for you. If you can pay it back sooner, great, if not, you won't default.
- Is this your only option? Be picky. If you can get one lender/Investor hooked, you can probably get others.

Bootstrapping Your Product

Here are three ways to bootstrap your way into new product development:

1. Work on your product at night and over the weekend while keeping your "day job".
2. Get current customers to fund research and development
3. Get customers who will be using the product to prepay for licenses or royalties.

Option 1: Find a Partner

Often, the best businesses are those that are started by two people of different backgrounds with different skills sets. You may be a marketing genius but know literate but knows nothing about business.

Together, you may make great team. Martha Stewart has a woman she works with named Sharon Patrick, a steady woman who helps run the empire. Martha likes to compare Ms. Patrick to Jeep-solid and dependable. Many Entrepreneurs need their own Jeep, yours just happens to be one who has money, that's all.

How to Find a Partner with Money

- Networking is essential. Put the word out to your lawyer, accountant, and banker that you are looking for a business partner.
- Speak with friends, family, colleagues and people where you worship. Word of mouth has found many partners.
- Speak also with suppliers and distributors for possible leads.
- People in your line of work who have retired may be interested in being either a working or silent partner.
- Look online. Try www.businesspartners.net.
- Advertise. Most classifieds sections of most newspapers have Capital Needed section. Also look under the Capital Available section.

Option 2: Distributor and Supplier Financing

Distributors and suppliers want your business. They want you to become a lucrative, repeat customer. As such, they know that one way to do that is to help start-up loan from a distributor or supplier is not out of the question. Given that it may even be possible to negotiate one against the other to see who will offer you the best deal. Your best bet is to focus on the largest suppliers in your field and make a sophisticated, professional pitch to them. Yet, who knows? It may be that a newer, smaller distributor may be more anxious to earn your business and will be more amenable to the pitch. When you are a bootstrapper, you have to be willing to fall down to succeed.

Option 3: Franchisor Financing

Finding a franchisor that will finance 50 percent or more of a franchise is very possible. According to the International Franchising Association, roughly 33 percent of all franchisors offer some type of financing. That means the franchisors will finance at least part (and sometimes all) of the franchisee's investment requirements. Franchisor loans can be structured a variety of ways. Some offer interest only loans with a balloon payment due in five years other offer loans that

How Supplier Financing Works

Before a supplier helps finance your business, it usually will visit your site, research your reputation, contact your bank, and call your references. It will want to be sure you are someone of honesty and integrity. Again, the key to success is preparation. An idea is not enough. Have a solid presentation ready that explains how your great business plan can benefit the supplier's bottom line. Show the need for your service or product.

One of the best things you can do is get some preorders and go back to the supplier and explain that you need financing to fill those orders. Require no payment at all for the first year. Some franchisors finance everything, while others offer loans for the franchise fee only. It all depends upon you and the franchisor, so you have to ask. Another option is that most franchisors work with banks and other lenders with whom they have long-established relations. These preferred lenders may also be able to help. Other franchisor alternatives, aside from direct financing, include loan guarantees or working capital. Finally, in addition to helping with the start-up costs, many franchisors usually have arrangements with leasing companies for the equipment needed to run the franchise. This can be a major expense, so don't overlook this possibility.

Option 4: Venture Capital Firms and Angel Investors

As discussed in earlier individuals who have made a lot of money often want to invest it. The main thing that these sorts of investors look at is the management team of the enterprise. They know that their investment is only as good as the people running the business.

Other things they will look at include:

- The ability to become highly profitable and dominate an industry.
- Strong leadership

- Experience, tenacity, commitment and integrity
- Innovation
- A great product

Option 5: Seller Financing

A final option for starting a business on a shoestring is to buy an established business and have the seller finance all or part of the purchase. Seller financing is actually quite common in the sale of small businesses. While there are many reasons for this, including lack of bank financing, seller financing is an option because it offers benefits for both the buyer and the seller. For the buyer, seller financing reduces the risk that the business is successful only because of the present owner's contacts or specialized knowledge.

If you wanted to buy a music store for example, there is a possibility some customers may not remain loyal without the long-established owner on the premises. But seller financing alleviates this fear. By having the seller finance part of the purchase price, it tells you that he believes the business can thrive on its own.

From a buyer's perspective, seller financing not only indicates that the seller believes in the business, but it also allows him or her to make a better offer for the business, which is good for the seller. It is likely that a seller will want the buyer to secure the purchase with some collateral. Just as a bank has the rights to fore close on a home if you default on the mortgage, business owners usually want to be able to "foreclose" on the business if you default. That is small price to pay though for the chance to buy into an established business. Seller financing may cost you a bit more, but overall, it can help both sides and should work out fine as long as both parties do their homework and deliver what is promised.

Don't Blow Your Dough on Rent

In order to start your business on a budget, every dollar you must have must be preserved and spent on only the most necessary items. As rent is often one of the biggest expenses a business has, it follows that you will be better able to start your business if you don't spend a lot of money on rent. If you do not need a high-profile location, don't get one. Start small; pick an inexpensive location, and move on to better digs after you are established. An even better option, as discussed earlier.

Another low-cost option is to start your business in a business incubator. The purpose of a business incubator, as the name suggests, is to foster and launch new business ventures and increase chances of success by providing low-cost space, overhead, administrative services, equipment and expertise. Run as nonprofit organizations, business incubators are usually started and funded by governments, universities or other groups that are interested in job creation and community economic development.

The difference between an incubator and shared space is that those who run incubators are dedicated to helping the businesses houses there succeed through in-house management, as well as financial and business consulting. If you are lucky enough to get your venture housed in a business incubator, be ready to get an informal MBA in the process. You will likely learn more about business than you thought possible.

While all business incubators have the same goal in mind -helping to launch successful businesses -each is unique in its own way because many incubators specialize. In the Silicon Valley, for example, you might find a business incubator that fosters high-tech businesses; in Iowa, the incubator may be farming oriented. It all depends upon the nature of the region and the mission of the particular incubator. The bad news about the business is twofold. First, not all incubators are created equal. Some are more successful at accomplishing their goals than others. Second, even if you are not in the best of incubators, you will nevertheless get spoiled. Subsidized rent, camaraderie, and free help are hard to be at. But because the point of a business incubator is to launch new businesses, you will have to move soon rather than later in order to make room for the next bootstrapping entrepreneur.

Fixtures and Equipnment

You do not need new fixtures or new equipment. Your business may look a bit nicer and cleaner, but when you are on a budget (and often, even when you are not), it simply is not worth the extra expense. Buying used can save you a lot of money, and it's even possible to get these things without paying anything up front by searching in the following places:

- **The Yellow Pages.** You will find several businesses that sell used fixtures and equipment. When companies remodel or go out of business, used equipment stores buy fixtures and equipment and, as they say, pass the savings on to you. These places usually have tons of used furniture, fixtures, display cabinets and other items that you may need to set up your business.
- **The internet.** One place to start is eBay, but there are also many other online auction houses, used business furnishings sites, and wholesale distributors that can help you equip your store for a bargain.

Growing Your Business without Big Bucks

If you are going to succeed in your small business, you must get people in the door, and that usually requires and advertising and marketing budget. The bootstrap start-up thus has a doubly daunting challenge: growing the business and so without a lot of money. Tough, yes, but it can be done.

Advertising on a Budget

Advertising is the lifeblood for many businesses, but to be effective, it must be done correctly. This is even more true when yours is a bootstrap business. There is no room for error. Accordingly, the first you must do is to analyze who your customers are, or who they are likely to be. If you don't know to whom you are selling, you won't know where to advertise in order to reach them. How old are they? Where do they come from? What are they looking for? Once you have a good idea of whom you are looking to attract with your advertising, you can earmark your ad money much more wisely and specifically. The trick is to find the right media source; that is, the one most frequented by your potential customers.

Buy unused time or space

If you call a magazine, newspaper, radio or television outlet near their and deadline, you may find that they have space they have not yet sold. this is called remnant place (for print media) or time (for the electronic media). Remnant buys are often available at a great discount.

Advertise in less traditional media outlets or at odd times

If your business will cater to teens, for example, buying an ad in a local alternative Newspaper is much cheaper than your local daily. This also true for electronic media. Buying an ad on television or radio is much less expensive if you advertise on smaller stations or in the middle of the night. Find out what they are asking and it is quite possible to pay less than the going rate if you walk in with cash and a commitment to pay less.

Get your ad produced more cheaply

You do not need to hire an expensive ad agency to create your ad. Be creative. Find a graphic artist who moonlights or approach a student at an art school to create an ad for you. Be willing to barter

Use Flyers

Flyers can advertise specials, offer discounts, grab attention, and best of all, be created very inexpensively on your computer.

Use door hangers

Hiring some local kids to distribute door hangers can be an inexpensive yet very effective way to bring in success.

Take out a classified ad

Daily and weekly newspaper, as well as local and national magazines, carries inexpensive classified ads, and the people who read them are often in the mood to buy something. Classified ads need to be clear and simple. It is best to offer only one product or service per ad.

Tap into regional papers

Newspapers and other publications often have regional editions that cost much less to advertise in than the regular edition.

Have visitors to your Website "subscribe"

Ask visitors to give you their e-mail address in order to get your content and make sure that you explain that their email addresses will be completely private. After that, send them to a special page on your site to sign up, and be sure to have an ad there for your product.

Motivating without Money

Your business is often only a good as your employees. if you want to increase sales, it is imperative that you have an energetic, motivated staff. How do you do that without spending a lot of money? The first thing to realize is that we all work for a variety of reasons, money being only one of them. Your job as an entrepreneur is to realize what other things motivate your employees and tap into those. Often, what people want out of work depends on their age. If you can understand the various motivating factors of different employees, you will be able to provide incentives for a job well done, and do so without raising salaries. the following details some of these groups and what each may be looking for.

PART V

RELEASING YOUR INCREASE

CHAPTER 28

Understanding The Principle
of Sowing And Reaping

*The natural seed that controls
your financial destiny is the
money you have now*

RELEASING YOUR INCREASE

"The path of a just is like the shining sun that shines
even brighter to the perfect."

Proverbs 4:18

"While the earth remaineth, seedtime and harvest and
cold and heat, and summer and winter, and day and
night time shall not cease"

Genesis 8:22

It is your destiny to increase with the passage of time. God expects you to
increase and become a great entrepreneur, great corporate person running
great successful business, company or organization. The first thing God
said to Adam and Eve was, be "fruitful and multiply." God has invested
a lot in nature that commands geometric progression, which is about
multiplication and no addition.

"And when your herds and your flocks multiply, and your silver and your gold are multiplied, and all that you have is multiplied."

Deuteronomy 7: 13

You can not be a child of a big God and remain a small child. Let thanksgiving proceed from you. He will multiply you and you will not diminish. You will progress and not regress. You will increase and not decrease. You cannot talk of fruitfulness, multiplication, greatness without seed sowing. It goes without saying that if you miss the planting season your harvest is not view.

The seed principle is powerful. There are different seeds: spiritual seeds, financial seeds and love seeds among others. For the purpose of this book I will concentrate on financial seeds. The natural seed that controls your financial destiny is the money you have now. The seeds of the present control the future. The law of multiplication or increase is a death and resurrection experience. Until your seed dies, it would not grow.

"Except a grain of wheat falls into the ground and dies, it abides alone, but if it dies it brings forth much fruit."

John 12:24

This is a call to invest in the right ground-business to realize the expected returns from investment. You reap what you sow Always understand that the kind of seed that you sow is the kind of harvest you will reap an idea. Dr. Robert Schuller said, sow a prayer and you will reap an idea. Many people do not receive the answers to their prayers because they do not understand what God gives from the realm of the spirit.

There is no money in heaven. They neither spend dollars nor any other currency there, so do not expect any to come from there.

"He that observes the wind will not sow, and he who regards the cloud will not reap."

Ecclesiastes 11:4

Do not let circumstances dictate what you should do. God did not leave it your feelings because he has already determined the seasons. Seed time and harvest time are determined.

RECEIVE THE GRACE TO SOW

"No man takes from me, but I lay it down of myself;
I have power to lay down and I have power to take it
again"

John 10:18

Until you have the power to lay it down you would not have the power to take it up because you did not sow anything. The destiny you are looking for is a harvest, what you have today is your seed. If you do not have the power (Finances) to lay down you will not have a harvest.

MONEY FLOWS IN THE DIRECTION OF POWER:

"You shall remember the Lord, your God because it is,
He that gives you the power to get wealth."

Deuteronomy 8:18

God won't give you cash directly. If you are looking for God to give you money, you are still operating at the lower level. All you need is power to command the flow of the cash. The power they get wealth. When you are blessed, people see the effect. When the things happen consistently in your lives that are that are positive, people know there must be something on you. The curse is the direct opposite of blessings. It produces negative results consistently in a person's life. It is the supernatural force that disrupts the ability to be prosperous. There is also something behind the person that gets good results the blessing, the power to get wealth. God told Abraham:

"I will make you a great nation, I will bless you and
make your name great and you shall be a blessing and

I will bless those who bless you and curse those who curse you. In you all the families of the earth shall be blessed."

Genesis 12:2-3

When you have the power to get wealth you will never be at a loss for great business ideas you need to get what you want. The anointing comes with wisdom.

CHAPTER 29

Harvesting

> *Be passionate in your giving*
> *to encounter high harvest*

HARVESTING is most often referring to selling a business or product line, as when a company sells a product line or division or a family sells a business. Harvesting is also occasionally used to refer to sales of product or product line towards the end of a product life cycle.

Harvesting is therefore a strategy in which investment in a particular line of business is reduced or eliminated because the revenue brought in by additional investment would not warrant the expense. A harvest strategy is employed when a line of business is considered to be a cash cow, meaning that the brand is mature and is unlikely to grow if more investment is added. The company will instead siphon off revenue that the cash cow brings in until the brand is no longer profitable. Simply put harvesting is a final phase in the entrepreneurial value creation process, which includes building, growing and harvesting. Harvesting is the process entrepreneurs and inventors use to exit a business and liquidate their investment in firm. While all three phases are important piece of the entrepreneurial process, many entrepreneurs who fail to execute a successful harvest do not realize the full benefits of their year of labor.

Harvesting is the means of capturing or unlocking value, reducing risk, and creating exit options. It is about more than money, as it also involves personal and non-financial considerations. As consequences, even upon realizing an acceptable monetary value for the firm, an entrepreneur who is not prepared for the lifestyle transition that accompanies the harvest may come away disappointed with the overall outcome. Thus, crafting a harvest strategy is essential to the entrepreneur's personal success as it is his or her financial success.

The message to the entrepreneur is this: the time to develop an effective harvest strategy is now, not later. As a firm moves toward the harvest, two questions regarding value are of primary importance. First are the current owners/managers creating value? You can harvest only what you have created.

CHAPTER 30

Divestment

> *The grass withers the flower fades, but*
> *the word of our God stands forever*

DIVESTMENT is a form of retrenchment strategy used by businesses when they downsize the scope of their business activities. Divestment usually involves eliminating apportion of a business. Firms may elect to sell, close, or spin –off a strategic business unit, major operating division, or product line. This move often is the final decision to eliminate unrelated, unprofitable, or unmanageable operations.

Divestment is commonly the consequence of growth strategy. Much of corporate downsizing has been the result of acquisitions and takeovers. Firms often acquired other business with operation in areas with which the acquiring firm had a little experience. After trying for a number of years to integrate the new activities into existing organization, many firms have elected to divest themselves of portions of business in order to concentrate on those activities in which they had a competitive advantage.

Reasons to divest

In most cases it is not immediately obvious that a unit should be divested. Many times, management will attempt to increase investment as a means of giving the unit of an opportunity to turn its performance around. Portfolio models such as the Boston Consulting Group [BCG] or General Electric's Business Screen can be used to identify operations in need of divestment. For example, products or business operations identified "as dogs in BCG model are prime candidates for divestment.

Decision to divest may be made for a number of reasons:

Market share too small:

Firms may divest where their market share is too small for them to be competitive or when the market is too small to provide the expected rates of return.

Availability of Better Alternatives:

Firms may also decide to divest because they see better investment opportunities. Organizations have limited resources. They are often able to divest resources from marginally profitable line of business to one where the same resources can be used to achieve a greater rate of return.

Need for increase investment:

Firms sometimes reach a point where continuing to maintain an operation is going to require a large investment in equipment, advertising, research and development and so forth to remain viable. Rather than invest the monetary and management resources, firms may elect to divest that portion of the business.

Lack of strategic fit:

A common reason for divesting is that the acquired business is not constant with the image and strategies of the firm. This can be result of acquiring a diversified business. It may also result from decisions to restructure and refocus the existing business.

Legal pressures to divest:

Firms may be forced to divest operations to avoid penalties for restraint of trade. Service Corporation Inc., a large funeral home chain acquired so many of its competitors in some areas that it created a regional monopoly.

Implementation of divestment strategies:

Firms may pursue a divestment strategy by spinning off a portion of the business and allowing it to operate as an independent business entity. Firms may also divest by selling a portion of the business to another organization. Another way to implement a divestment decision is to simply close apportion of the firms operations.

Many divestments are blocked by management's expectations for the operation. Firms may expect demand for the product to pick up. Management may also see the poor performance as a temporary setback that can be overcome with the time and patience. Decisions to divest a business may also be seen as admission of failure on the part of management and may lead to escalating commitment to the struggling business as a way of protecting management's ego and public image.

Divestment is not usually the first choice of strategy for a business. However, a product demand changes and firms alter their strategies, there will almost always be ome portion of neither the business that is nor performing to management's expectations. Such operation is a prime target for divestment and may well leave the company in stronger competitive position if it is divested.

CHAPTER 31

Succession Planning

SUCCESSION PLANNING is a process of identifying and developing internal people with the potential to fill key business leadership positions in the company. Succession planning increases the availability of experienced and capable employees that are prepared to assume these roles are they become available. Taken narrowly, "replacement planning" for key roles is the heart of succession planning.

Effective succession or talent-pool management concerns itself with building a series of feeder groups up and down the entire leadership pipeline or progression. In contrast, replacement planning is focused narrowly on identifying specific backup candidates for the given senior management positions. For the most part position-driven replacement planning (often referred to as the" truck scenario") is forecast, which research indicates does not have substantial impact on outcomes.

Fundamental to succession-management process is an underlying philosophy that argues that top talent in corporation must be managed for the greater good of the enterprise. Merck and other companies argue that a "a talent mindset" must be part of a leadership culture for these practices to be effective.

Succession planning is a process whereby an organization ensures that employees are recruited and developed to fill each key role within the company. Through your succession planning process, your recruit superior employees, develop their knowledge, skills and abilities and prepare them for advancement or promotion into ever more challenging roles. Actively pursuing succession planning ensures that employees are constantly developed to fill each needed role. As your organization expands, loses key employees, provides promotional opportunities, and increase sales, your succession planning guarantees that you have employees on hand ready and waiting to fill new roles. According to 2006 Canadian federation of independent business survey, slightly more than on third of independent business owners plan to exit their business within the next 5 years and within the next 10 years two thirds of owners plan to exit their business. the survey also found that small and medium sized enterprise are not adequately prepared for their business succession: only 10% owners have formal, written succession plan; 38% have an informal, written plan and the remaining 52% do not Have Any Succession Plan At All. the results are backed by 2004 CIBC survey which suggests that succession planning is increasingly becoming a critical issue. By 2010, CIBC estimates that 1.2 million USA dollars in business assets are poised to change hands.

Research indicates may succession-planning initiatives fall short of their intent (corporate leadership council 1998). "Bench strength" as it is commonly called, remains a stubborn problem is many if not most companies. Studies indicates that companies that report the greatest gains from succession planning feature high ownership by CEO and high degree of engagement among the larger leadership team.

Research indicates that clear objectives are critical to establishing effective succession planning. These objectives tend to be core to many or most companies that have well established practices: identify those with the potential to assume greater responsibility in the organization; provide critical development experiences to those that can move into key roles; engage the leaders ;build a data base that can be used to make better staffing decisions for key jobs, in other companies these additional objectives may be embedded in the succession process; improve employee commitment and retention ; meet the career development expectation of existing employees and counter the increasing difficulty and cost of recruiting employees externally.

SUCCESSION PLANNING WITH YOUR BOARD

Succession planning is a means for an organization to ensure its continued effective performance through leadership continuity. For an organization to plan for the replacement of key leaders, potential leaders must first be identified and prepared to take on those roles. It is not enough to select people in the organization who seem "right" for the job. Not only should the experience and duties be considered, but also the personality, the leadership skill, and readiness for taking on a key leadership role.

Next determine which members to consider for the leadership positions. It is best to identify this group with an objective system instead of just selecting "favorites." One option is for members to self –select into process. This way, those who are already interested in the leadership roles will volunteer. They may be the most likely to take it seriously. Several "hopeful" should be identified for each position to be filled. This allows the potential leaders to be "groomed", trained and mentored for the possibility of filling the leadership positions. When the time comes for the position to be filled there will be several people from which to choose, all of whom have had the time to develop for new roles. At least one of them may be ready to meet the requirements.

In order to prepare potential leaders, the gap between what they are ready for now and what preparation they need to be ready for the job when it is available needs to be determined. This information can help determine what training, experience, and mentoring is needed. By considering their past performance and volunteer, past experience, fit with the organizational culture and other members' acceptance of them as potential leaders, the best to fit can be determined. Also, ensure that the potential leaders are willing to carry out organization's mission and to continue the organization's philosophy and culture.

Once the potential leaders have been identified, a plan for each of them should be developed. Each potential leader should be assigned a mentor, this mentor; this mentor should be the person whom they may replace. The mentor and the potential leader should form a teacher-student relationship. When issues arise that need problem solving or decision making, the leader should meet with the potential leader to ask how he or she would handle the situation.

Allow the potential leaders to "shadow" the leaders. If possible, allow them to attend board meetings and participate in the decision making. This is a great way to see how they problem solve and interact.

These leaders may even want to present the potential leaders with a problem and allow them to solve it as a group without any benefit of the leaders' input. See if the potential leaders would react in a way that is suitable or favorable.

Also allow them to participate in goal-setting activities, such as strategic planning or budgeting. Is it important to see them in action? This process should not be a means for the leaders to choose the person most like them. Because a potential leader solves problems the same way as the leader does not make him or her best candidate.

The board may want to plan to conduct interviews with each candidate, assessing his or her abilities to make decisions, solve problems, behave appropriately in sensitive and lead those who will report to him or her. If appropriate, it is a good idea to allow direct reports to have some say in who will lead them.

Finally, evaluate the succession planning efforts. What went well? What went wrong? What could be done differently? Make suggestions and recommendations for improving the process so that it runs more smoothly next time. If all goes as planned the succession planning process will ensure a smooth transition and a new leader who is prepared for his or her role in the organization.

SUCCESSION PLANNING PROCESS

This following steps should be followed: determine the key leaders for whom successors will be identified; identify the competencies of current key leaders; identify experience and duties required; identify personality, political savvy, judgment; identify leadership skills, select the high-potential members who will participate in succession planning; identify gap between what the high-potential members are able to do presently and what they must do in the leadership role; create a development plan for a each high-potential member to prepare him or her for the leadership position; perform development activities with each-high potential member; interview and select a member for the new leadership position and evaluate succession planning efforts and make changes to program based on evaluation for future programs.

BUSINESS EXIT PLANNING

With the global proliferation of small and mid-sized enterprises (SME's, issues of business succession and continuity have become increasingly common. When the owner of a business becomes incapacitated healthy business, which is forced into bankruptcy because of lack of available liquidity to avoid many of the problems associated with succession and transfer of ownership.

Business Exit Planning is a body of knowledge which began development in the United States toward the end of the 20th century, and is now spreading globally. A Business Exit Planning exercise begins with the shareholder (s) of a company defining their objectives with respect to an eventual exit, and the executing their plan, as the following definitions suggest:

Business Exit Planning is the process of explicitly defining exit-related objectives for the owners of a business, followed by the design of a comprehensive strategy and road map that take into account all personal, business, financial, legal, and taxation aspects of achieving those objectives, usually in the context of planning the leadership succession and continuity of a business. Objectives may include maximizing (or setting a goal for) proceeds, maximizing risk, closing a Transaction quickly' or selecting an investor that will ensure that the business that prospers. The strategy should also take into account contingencies such as illness or death.

All personal and business aspects should be taken into consideration. This is also a good time to plan an efficient transfer from the point of view of possibly applicable estate taxes, capital gains taxes, or other taxes.

Sale of a business is not the only form of exit. Forms of exit may also include initial public Offering, management Buyout, passing on the firm to next-of-kin, or even bankruptcy. Bringing on board financial strategic or financial partners may also be considered a form of exit, to the extent that it may help ensure succession and survival of the business.

In developed countries, the so-called "baby boomer" demo-graphic wave is now reaching the stage where serious considers action needs to give to exit. Hence, the importance in the coming years.

FAMILY BUSINESS

Arieu proposed a model in order to classify family into four scenarios: political, openness, foreign management and natural succession.

POLITICAL SCENARIO: this is the case of a company linked to a large family, where it is expected that through inheritance, the property would spray quickly, possibly faster than the growth of own business, resulting in a dividend per head lower and lower. Identifying suitable member in the family can incorporate to address and possibly distinguish who may occupy the general direction afterwards.

However, the existence of many members in the family can turn into conflicts of power, making it necessary to establish agreements and occasionally reorganize the business in terms of those individuals who, because of the obvious professional and human qualities can be recognized to create new companies and business units.

OPENESS: when members of the next generations are numerous and among them is not possible to identify a person who possesses the characteristics necessary to assume leadership positions with expertise in family business, we have a scenario that we call open, since the strategy more suitable for this type of organization is to shift some capital to others who can provide not only management skills but also liquidity for business, creating more value for society and retention of jobs avoid future complications.

FOREIGN MANAGEMENT: this scenario occurs when family members who control the business are not many, and yet, not having any of its members with a natural profile of leadership succession when they choose to appoint a non-family CEO.

NATURAL SUCCESSION: families seeking to preserve its legacy business are the most favorable conditions in the presence of a stage natural succession. This is the case of accompany controlled by a few families, few heirs who in turn have identified among them a worthy successor, a strong name also is associated with the adequacy to drive its growth, the ability to run the organization, understanding market and committeeman which means only a part of the family patrimony is also a source of value to society, other shareholders, customers, suppliers and even their own employees (stakeholders). This will help in improved succession planning.

PROCESS AND PRACTICES

Companies devise elaborate models to characterize their succession and development practices. Most reflect a cyclical series of activities that include these fundamentals.

- Identify key roles for succession or replacement planning
- Define the competencies and motivational profile required to undertake those roles.

- Assess people against these criteria's – with future orientation.
- Identify pools of talent that could potentially fill and perform highly in key roles.
- Develop employees to be ready for advancement into key roles – primarily through the right set of experiences.

In many companies, over the past several years, the emphasis has shifted from planning job assignment to development, with much greater focus on managing key experiences that are critical to growing global business leaders. North American companies for example tend to be more active in this regard followed by European and Latin American countries.

Pepsi Co, IBM and Nike are current examples of the so-called "game planning" approach to succession and talent management. In these and other companies annual reviews are supplemented with an ongoing series of discussion among senior leader about who is ready to assume larger roles.

Vacancies are anticipated and slates of names are prepared based on highest potential and readiness for job moves. Organization realignments are viewed as critical windows of opportunity to create development moves that will serves the greater of the enterprise.

Assessment is a key practice in effective succession planning. There is no widely accepted formula for evaluating the future potential of leaders, but there are many tools and approaches that continue to be used today, arranging from personality and cognitive testing to team-based interviewing and simulations and other assessment center methods. Elliott Jaques and other have argued for the importance of focusing assessment narrowly on critical on critical differentiators of future performance. Jaques developed a persuasive case for measuring candidate' ability to manage complexity, formulating a rebuts operational definition of business intelligence. The cognitive process profile (CPP) psychometric is an example of a tool used in succession planning to measure candidates' ability to manage complexity according to Jaques' definition.

Companies struggle to find practices that are effective and practical. It is clear leaders who rely on instinct and gut to make promotion decision are often not effective. Research indicated that most valid practices for assessment are those "calibration meeting." Composed of senior leaders can be quite effective judging a slate of potential senior leaders with the right tool and facilitation.

With organization facing increasing complexity and uncertainty in their operation environment some suggest a move away from competences based approaches. In a future that is increasingly hard to predict leaders will need to see opportunity in volatility, spot patterns in complexity, find creative solutions to problems, keep in mind long term strategic goals for the organization and wider society, and hold onto uncertainty until the optimum time to make a decision.

Professionals in the field, including academics, consultants and corporate practitioners, have many strongly held views on the topic. Best practice is a slippery concept in this field. There are many thought pieces on the subject that readers may find valuable such as "Debunking 10 Top Talent Management Myths," talent management magazines, Doris Sims, and December 2009. Research-based writing is more difficult to find the Corporate Leadership Council. The Best Practice Institute (BPI) and the Center for Creative Leadership, as well as the Human Resources Planning Society are sources of some effective research-based materials.

Over the years, Organization has changed their approach to succession planning. What used to be a rigid? Confidential process of hand-picking executives to be company successors in now becoming a more fluid, transparent practice that identifies high-potential leaders and incorporates development programs preparing them for top positions. Today, corporations consider succession planning a part of a holistic strategy called **"talent management"**

According to the company PEMCO, talent management is defined as the activities and processes throughout the employee life cycle: recruiting and hiring, on boarding, training, professional development, performance management, workforce planning, leadership development, career development, the employee exit process". When managing internal talent, companies must "know whether the right people, are moving at the right place into the right jobs at the right time" an effective succession planning strategy, coupled with solid career development programs, will help paint a more promising future for employees.

Development goals have been achieved.

People fluent succession planning software helps businesses build a sustainable leadership pipeline through internal talent development and recruiting.

Features include:

- Interactive succession planning charts and talent profile to view the readiness of potential successors for key position.
- "Extended enterprise" succession features that optionally extends the succession planning process outside the organization.
- A talent profile hub that captures historical performance management data for easy reference.
- Tools for employees to research career opportunities and express interest within the talent profile.

Silkroad wingspan managers all employee information compiled from assessments, appraisals, goals and development plans so that HR can automatically classify internal candidates for a given position.

Features include:

- Career development tools that highlight the skills to be acquired by each employee, and the anticipated time to complete development goals.
- Comparison tools that allows for views of all potential candidate side by side while adjusting job-specific criteria.
- Separate modules that can operate individually or as an integrated employee performance management system.

LOOK OUT

Companies make many mistakes when it comes to succession planning. Here are the most common-and how to avoid them.

1. Using the past to plan for the future: you need to choose leaders whose skills align with future goals. To avoid this trap, make sure succession plans align with the long-term strategic vision of the business.
2. Stopping at the CEO: the best succession planning programs at least address the entire leadership team as well as senior management: "succession planning is a multi-person event," schooley says. "If

one person moves up, it creates a new hole that can ripple through the organization."

3. Not getting the Board on board: CEOs and HR often think they have a succession plan in place only to discover the board disagrees. : it's a big mistake to assume the viability of a candidate in your mind without vetting it with the board," Miles says. The best programs incorporate the board of directors in planning and keep them up-to-date on development efforts to ensure everyone is on the same page.

4. Allowing human capital roadblocks to take root: When talented people top out in leadership roles, they can prevent the next generation from moving up. The best companies avoid these roadblocks by creating new positions, collaboration opportunities and stretch assignment so future leaders have room to grow.

5. Succession isn't part of the culture. Succession planning fails when there is no incentive for executives to mentor their people, Schneider says. Best-of-breed companies encourage executives to identify and develop talented young leaders and align their compensation with these efforts. "It should be considered a badge of honor to have your people selected for promotion.

6. The wrong people making decision. CEOs aren't in the best position to choose their successor, because they often are more focused on their current legacy than the company's future goals. The best companies involve HR and the board when making succession planning decisions.

We've organized this roadmap into three phases to help you implement the planning and execution of you succession planning program. Below is summary of the "plan," "Do" and "review" of succession planning.

PLAN

- How deep you want to go: Just the C-suite? Management? Everyone?
- Determine whether you will focus on high potential workers or extend succession planning to a wider pool of employees.

- Define the skills and experience needed for key roles: Think about where the company is going and what leadership skills you'll need to get there.
- Evaluate whether your HR software offers succession planning tool and whether you want to use them.

DO

- Assess employees' current performance and identify any skill or experience gaps for their future roles.
- Ask employees about their career goals so you are certain they want the role you are grooming them for.
- Create training, mentoring and leadership opportunities for top talent to close the gaps.
- Work with the CEO and the board to create a list of two to three candidate for every top position.

REVIEW

- Review assessment of top talent with the board every nine to 15 months, and again whenever there is major change in relationship.
- Identity development roadblocks-such as lack of mentors or limited on-the-job leadership opportunities-and look for solution.
- Review succession plans during annual strategic planning, to ensure development goals align with strategic goals.
- Be willing to adapt the succession planning list if your goals change, or if individual employees aren't showing the leadership development you need.

Conclusion

Starting and Growing a Successful Great Business is Possible

Our greatest growing up every time fairly is not in never failing but in risky

IN THE COURSE OF THIS BOOK you have learned many things about to start and grow a successful great business. You have learned the business growth strategies and how to implement them. Since you now know what it takes start and grow a successful great business the next step is to learn how to apply all of the information that you have learned from this book to your own personal situation. That might of course be very intimidating and I stress and fully recommend that you use own mentor to help you go through this process. This process is the practical application and implementation of what you have learned in this book put into action in your own life. By that I mean you need to make a decision on what you want to accomplish and determine the best way for you to accomplish that goal.

Let me point out that an idea of to start and grow a successful great business I possible. Success is not a matter of luck or accident or being in the right place at the right time. Success is possible and by practicing what you have just learned, you will move to the frontline in life and with no doubt you are relocating to the top as a champion in your own area and from today you will not scratch with turkeys but eagles. You will have an age over those that who do not know or do not practice these techniques and strategies.

If you consistently do the things that other successful people do, nothing in the world can stop you from becoming a great successful yourself. You are now the architect of your own destination. You are behind the steering wheel of your own life.

YOU NOW HAVE TO GIVE IT ALL IT TAKES!

And say to Archippus, take heed to the ministry which thou hast received in the Lord, that thou fulfill it that you have received a ministry from the Lord doesn't guarantee its fulfillment or that you will excel in it

Colossians 4:7

"Take heed" means get to know what it takes and give it all it takes to fulfill the ministry of assignment you have received from the Lord". It is my prayer that you put all you have learned from it to work. Also, it is important to know that you can no attain Excellency in any assignment or business which you have not received from the Lord. This is because God is not committed to what he has not commanded.

I have not sent these prophets yet they ran: I have not spoken to them, yet they prophesied

Jeremiah 23:21

So, if the vision is to from the Lord, you will be the one to power and fund it. But if it is from him, then all you need to do is to simply position yourself and do what he tells you to do. Therefore, do not make ambitions, passion and impression for a vision. Now that you have been many tools in this book, you can use these tools to reach your goal and help you accomplish what you see to achieve. You see as a millionaire or a billionaire business or manager or leader and you are always looking for new opportunities to make money and you are always looking to develop business to the next level, but if you are using the tools and knowledge that you develop in the beginning you can also apply to those strategies to all future businesses.

So even if this book didn't give you a specific answer or a specific piece of advice on exactly what type of business you should start or how you should run your business, what this book has given you are the tools to be able to learn on own your own as far as what type of business you should start, run and grow.

Wherefore the rather, brethren, give diligence to make your calling and election: for if ye do these things ye shall never fall.

2 Peter 1:10

Many have received very true visions from the Lord, but it does not seem to coming true, and they are wondering, "Could it be the lord has spoken?" yes it could be ordained by the Lord but they are requirements you must meet to fulfill that vision and make it work. These requirements are strategies that should be backed up with strategic capability. Any strategy without resources is bound to fail.

Lastly, your future is where you are going to take the big step of either starting a successful great business or even now if you are already involved in a business you are going to take everything that you have learned from this book to run your great business the same way a millionaire or billionaire businesses. Learn to know how to spot opportunities in the market place, and then learn how to develop opportunities that exist in the market place and you will be in charge of your destiny.

References

Books

Aaker, D. A. (2001), Strategic Market Managing, 6th ed. (New Jersey: John Wiley & Sons, Inc)

Aqualiano, N. (2001) Operational Management (New Jersey: McGraw-Hill Companies, Inc)

Bearden, L. (1990), 'Five Imperatives for improving service quality' (Great Brain: Ashford Color Press)

Boyett, J. and Boyett J. (1998), the Guru Guide (New Jersey: John Wiley &Sons, Inc)

Buswell, D. (1896), The development of quality measurement system for a UK Bank (London: Phillip Allan Oxford Press)

Blue's Clues for Success: The 8 Secrets Behind a phenomenal Business by Diane Tracy (Dearborn, 2002).

Chandler, A. (1992) Strategy and Structure (Great Britain: MIT Press)

Charan, R and Tichy, N. (1999), Every Business is Growth Business: How your Company Can Prosper year after year (New Jersey: McGraw-Hill Companies, Inc)

Church, G. (1999), Market Research: Methodological Foundation, 7th ed. (London)

Cox, K. and Kotler P. (1998), marketing, Managing and Strategy: 4th ed. (New Jersey: Prentice Hall, Inc).

Cohen, D, and Prusak, L. (2001), "How to Invest in social Capital" Haward Business Review Volume 79 no.6 pp 86-95

Cole G. A. (1997) Management Theory and Practice, (Great Britain: Ashford Color Press, Gosport)

D, Aven R. (2002), "The Empire Strikes Back- Counter Revelatory Strategies for industry Leaders" Harvard Business Review, Volume 80, no.11, pp 69-79

Daniels, J.2004, International Business, 9 USA: Pearson Education Limited)

David, F. R (2001), Strategic Management-Concepts and Cases 8th ed. (New Jersey: Practice Hal, Inc)

Doyley, P. (2002) Marketing Management ad Strategy, 3rd ed. (USA: Pearson Education Limited)

Duck, J. (1993:109), Managing Change: The Art of balancing, Harvard Business Review August.

East, r.(1997), consumer Behaviour: Advances and Application in Marketing (London : Prentice hall,Inc)

Ellis, G. (2007), Zero to Million: How to build a company to one million Dollars in sales (New Jersey: McGraw-Hills Companies, Inc)

Gerson, R. (1994), Measuring Customers Satisfaction (London: Keagan Keagan Limited)

Guerrilla Marketing Secrets for Marketing Big Profits from Your Small Business by Jay Conrad Lenvison (Mariner books, 1998).

Harrigan, K, and Porter, M, (1983), "End -Game Strategies for declining Industries" Harvard Business Review, July August.

Hisrich, R.(1998) Entrepreneurship, (USA:McGraw-Hill Companies, Inc)

Jeffrey,G. (2001:175), Journal of Business Venture, Harvard Business Review, July

Jones,G.(2005) How to launch and grow the new business, (Great Britain: Bell & Bain Ltd)

Karakaya, F, (2002), "Barriers to Entry in industrial Markets" Journal of Business and Industrial marketing, Vol.17 Issue 5

Lash, L. M. (1920), "care in service Business" Business and Finance Review, pp26-30

Laura, M.(1996), Bulding Adaptive Firm, Small Business Forum (Great Britain :Belll& Bain Lt)

McDonald, M. (1990), Marketing plans: How to prepare them, How to use them, 4th ed (USA)

McConnell, C.R and Brue, S.L (2002). Economics (New Jersey: McGraw-Hill Companies, Inc)

McHugh M. (2001), Understanding Business, (USA: McGraw-Hill Companies, Inc)

Melkam, A. (1979), How To handle Major Customers Profitably (USA: Butter Heinemann)

Nellis,J. (2004), Essence of Business Economics (India: Prentice Hall Private Limited)

Nickles, W. McHugh, J, et,al (2005), Understanding Business New York: McGraw-Hill Companies, Inc)

Oakland, J, (2001), Total Organizational Excellence- Achieving World-Class Performance (USA: Butterworth-Heinemann)

Olson, P. (1993), "Entrepreneurship start-up and growth, business and finance review, pp5-20

Own your own corporation; why the rich own their own companies and everyone else work for them by garret Sutton, Robert T

Pardo. C, 1999 account management in business-to-business field; A French overview' journal of business industrial marketing volume 14 issue 4.

Peter, M.[1998],'how competitive forces shape stratagem Harvard business review March to April.

Portraits of success; Nine keys to sustaining values in business by James Olan Hutchenson (Dearborn, 2002)

Potter D.(1999), "success under fire :policies to prosper in hustle time" Califofnia management review,winter,PP24-28

Radebaugh, L. (2002), international business (USA: McGraw hill companies inc)

Registrar of companies' data bank (2008)

Rigby, D. (2002) Moving upwards in downturn; Harvard business review vol. 80 no. 11 pp 99- 105

Robbins's, (2001), Organizational behavior (New Jersy; Prentice hall business review volume 81 no 3 pp52-59

Saunders M, Lewis P et Al (2003) Effective small business (USA, Pearson education limited)

Schumpeter, J, (1996) an intrinsic desire to succeed, (USA; Pearson education limited)

Spencer R (1999),Key Accounts effectively managing strategic complexity journal of business an industrial marketing,Vol 14 Issue 4

Stalk G. stern, c (1998) perspective on strategy from the Boston consulting group(USA;John Wiley and sons inc)

Stevenson (2005), operations management (New York; Mc Graw-Hill companies inc)

Sullivan, D(2001),international business (USA;Pearsoneducatin limited)

Wilson, D, (1993) Interpreneurships requisite area if development; A survey of top executives in successful entrepreneurial firm journal of venture (March 1993)

Zimmer T (2002) An entrepreneurial approach, (USA: McGraw-Hill companies inc)

Magazines and Newspapers

Black Enterprise <www.blackenterprise.com
Business 2.0 <www.business2.com
Business Startups<www.entrepreneur.com
Business week<www.buainessweek.com
Entrepreneur<www.entrepreneur.com
Fast Company www.fastcompany.com
Forbes<www.forbes.com
www.fortune.com
Franchise Handbook www.franchise1.com
Harvard Business Review <www.harvardbusinessonline.com
Inc.www.inc.com
Red Herring<www.redherring.com
Wall Street Journal<www.wsj.com

Other Websites

www.MrAllBiz.com
business.lycos.com
smalllbusiness.yahoo.com
www.aarpsmallbiz.com
www.about.com /smallbusiness
www.asbdc-us.org
www.att.sbresources.com
www.bcentral.com
www.bizland.com
www.bloomberg.com
www.business.gov
www.busop1.com
www.chamberbiz.com
www.entreworld.cm
www.isquare.com
www.onlinewbc.gov
www.quicken.com/smallbusiness
www.sba.gov
www.score.org
www.usatoday/money/smallbusiness/front.htm
www.winwome.org
www.workz.com

Printed in the United States
by Baker & Taylor Publisher Services